# FIRESTARTERS:

## For The Seasons of Our Life

# FIRESTARTERS:

## For The Seasons of Our Life

Pearl, Door & Mountain!

Fr. Ben

**Rev. Benjamin Berinti**

Rev. Benjamin Berinti

Outskirts Press, Inc.
Denver, Colorado

The opinions expressed in this manuscript are solely the opinions of the author and do not represent the opinions or thoughts of the publisher. The author has represented and warranted full ownership and/or legal right to publish all the materials in this book.

Firestarters:
For The Seasons of Our Life

V3.0



Outskirts Press, Inc.
http://www.outskirtspress.com

ISBN: 978-1-4327-6944-4



PRINTED IN THE UNITED STATES OF AMERICA

With deep love for my parents
Benjamin Peter and Bernadine Ann Berinti

In gratitude for 25 years of priestly ministry in the
Missionaries of the Most Precious Blood
June 22, 1985

# TABLE OF CONTENTS

# ACKNOWLEDGMENTS

*"I have come to set the earth on fire,*
*and how I wish it were already blazing!"*
*(Luke 12:49 NAB)*

I am grateful to all those who have kindled fires throughout the journey of my life. At times the fires have warmed, motivated, lighted the way, amazed...and even been like burning bushes where God's presence has truly been known. In return, I hope that I have also ignited a few fires to enkindle the hearts of others.

This collection of essays is but a fraction of spiritual reflections that I have crafted over the past 15 years of ministry. They first appeared as spiritual kindling for parishioners at St. Andrew Catholic Church, Orlando, Florida, and the Catholic Church of the Nativity, Longwood, Florida. Now they become available for a wider audience.

People who have come to know me over these 25 years of priestly ministry recognize that at any moment of our relationship and encounters, there may arise some experience that will eventually become the springboard for an essay, a homily, or a spiritual reflection. This is part of the risk of knowing me! And then there are those others, who unbeknownst to them, they have become a part of the fabric of my life as I have observed them from a distance. This simply is a testimony to the connection we all share as creatures of a loving and compassionate God, a God who knows what we need and who we need at any moment of our life. I am grateful for all these encounters and pray they may now become a source of blessing for those who share these "Firestarters".

I am particularly grateful for my parents, grandparents and special friends who have nurtured and nourished my own spiritual life journey. With gratitude for all that you have graciously shared with me, in your honor I share the embers of my own spiritual insights in the hopes that the Lord's great desire for a blazing world, raging with love and compassion and reconciliation might become a reality.

While these essays are gathered around specific "seasons" of the year, they can surely be enjoyed "out of season," as our lives do not always follow the marks on a calendar.

# ADVENT

*If we stop only for a moment and allow ourselves a quiet space amidst the pre-Christmas din, we will hear the voices of Advent calling out to us. They are the voices the world often tries to silence, yet the voices of Advent return each year to penetrate the loud, brash voices of distress and distraction. They are like soft, tender shoots reaching forth through a late Spring snow, gently reminding those who have eyes to see and ears to hear that new life is always below the cold, hard surface. As God's people, we are once again invited to enter a space where we can allow these Advent voices to percolate to the surface of our lives, to allow these voices to speak to us of God and the promises God has faithfully honored throughout all generations.*

# ONE LITTLE DOOR AND WINDOW AT A TIME....

I might be one of the few people in the United States who doesn't get all sappy about watching *It's A Wonderful Life!* Up until a few years ago, there wasn't a moment during the days preceding Christmas that a person couldn't turn to at least one channel on the tube and find oneself in the midst of another rerun of the movie. In fact, there were times when this "classic" was running simultaneously on several stations! Alas, this is no longer the case (I'll withhold my spontaneous desire to applaud; after all, it messes up my typing cadence!). The fans of *It's A Wonderful Life*, much to their chagrin, have been suffering ever since someone bought the corporate rights to the movie and only makes it available at their whim during the pre-Christmas season. For the true-blue fans of the film, I'm sure this occurrence illustrates yet another giant tug on the already unraveling moral fiber of our nation (surely, yet another diatribe for Bill O'Reilly)! Of course, in this beautiful world of ours, there's always the DVD version to snuggle up with.

Before anyone starts pelting me with snowflakes from the streets of Bedford Falls, and before you mistake me for a "Bah humbug" kind of guy, I am not against "sappy" Christmas programs altogether. In fact, I have a few of my own favorites. Unfortunately, no reruns are aired nor are there any DVDs of one of my favorites—*Dean Martin and the Golddiggers' Family Christmas Special!* (Just kidding....) Actually, I'm still partial to the umpteenth airings of *A Charlie Brown Christmas, Rudolph, Frosty, How the Grinch Stole Christmas* (the non-Jim Carey one), and *The Christmas Story* (with little Ralphie chasing the dream of his "Red Rider BB Gun"). Now, *these* are the classics from my youth, and I could watch them into nirvana.

A week or so ago, a modern "classic" (in our day, anything that airs more than two years in a row is called a "classic") of the pre-Christmas television indulgence was showing, and with nothing better to do, or should I say, with nothing better I *wanted* to do, I snuggled down to watch Chevy Chase's *Christmas Vacation.* I will be the first to admit that Chevy Chase is no Jimmy Stewart, but the film has its merits—it's just as sappy as the others! One of the touching little images running through the show, as the Griswold family struggles to enjoy an "old-fashioned family Christmas" (replete with all the normal disasters that befall families attempting to have an "old-fashioned" anything), was the opening of the little doors and windows of the Christmas house that marked off each of the calendar days approaching the great holiday.

Seeing that "Christmas Calendar" counting down the days, I was reminded of the many and varied Advent-Christmas calendars I encountered as a child, each with their small doors and windows to be opened as those pregnant days passed leading up to Christmas. The whole enterprise helped heighten the sense of anticipation, wonder, and curiosity already present in my preparations for Christmas. One never knew what would be behind the door or window—some pertinent words or a touching biblical scene from Holy Scripture, a smiling angel, admonitions to do specific good deeds before Christmas (always a key concern prior to Santa's arrival); there were even calendars with cold, hard cash residing behind some doors or windows (although, I quickly learned that these coins were meant only for show, and not for taking, as they had been GLUED to the page)!

In my reminisces about this tradition, which had its genesis in Germany (where we also get our traditions of the Christmas pine and lighted wreaths), I marveled at the simple, yet profound symbolism contained in these decorated pieces of cardboard.

**Isn't the process of gradually opening a piece of ourselves the whole purpose of Advent?**

Isn't the desire to make some small opening in our lives, so as to receive more fully the presence of Emmanuel, God-With-Us, the thrust of why we celebrate Christmas? Are not joy, excitement, anticipation, and curiosity some of the hallmark emotions one experiences in coming to know the Lord? The ability to embrace with a deeper appreciation and understanding exactly what it means to believe that God came to earth and made God's home with us is not something we can acquire all at once; it is not a once-for-all achievement. The power of this belief, this faith, is too overwhelming a reality to swallow in one giant gulp, and so it comes to us in small doses—one little door and window at a time.

At times, we are hard on ourselves because we do not embrace the love of God and the Gospel of Jesus Christ with unparalleled devotion and commitment. How often I hear people say: "I don't pray enough; I don't go to Mass every day or every Sunday; I'm not always compassionate with my family; I can't seem to totally accept the will of God in my life; I just don't understand everything the Church teaches." While we are certainly called to on-going conversion and growth in our faith, we simply cannot do it all, embrace it all, understand it all, and be secure in it all. "Perfection," while clearly an attribute that many of us strive for, or even pretend that we can create in our lives (and the lives of others), is a trait reserved only to God. With us, however, it is the *imperfection* of one little door and window at a time—one day at a time.

During these remaining Advent days, in this season of "openings," as we open our homes to family and friends (and maybe even strangers), as we open the gifts that we exchange, as we open the cards that bring warmth and friendship across the miles, as we open our eyes to the wonder and awe of the beauty of our still-aching world, as we open our ears to the sounds of the season, as we open our hands to giving beyond what we're usually accustomed to give...***may we open our lives to the God-of-Surprises, God-With-Us, who is waiting for us—one little door and window at a time.***

# DANCING WITH ADVENT SHADOWS

*There shall come forth a shoot from the stump of Jesse,*
*and a branch shall grow out of his roots.*
*In that day the root of Jesse shall stand as an*
*ensign to the peoples; him shall the nations seek,*
*and his dwellings shall be glorious. (Isaiah 11:1.10)*

Weeks before the night would fall on the first Advent Vigil, I spent pieces of several days simply sitting in our church, taking in the expanses of our worship environment. As I entered the spaces of the sanctuary and assembly with my eyes, I tried to bring my spirit along with them. My imagination began to play with visions for the upcoming season of Advent, wondering how we might be called as a community into a deeper, richer, more moving experience of worship through the profoundly stirring symbols leaping forth from the Advent scriptures. Oh yes, there is the "standard fare" of symbols replicated, often without much thought or grace, in churches everywhere. But how could we, a community of complexity, re-envision our space so as to create an environment that would welcome us into the mysteries of this blessed season?

The premier spokesperson of the season, the prophet Isaiah, sets before us a plethora of images—sights and sounds and visions, a feast too sumptuous to be savored in such a short number of weeks. Yet, as I stared at the expansive wall to the left of the altar and font, from the myriad of Isaiah-imagery, sprung forth a vision of the root—the root of Jesse, stretching forth from a stump—wispy, scraggly, wild, forceful, aching to be reborn into a living tree, aching with the pangs of pregnant desire for growth and rejuvenation. This root of Jesse, coming to life in my mind's eye, at once became united with the beautiful "vine and branches" of John's Gospel.

Imagination is a wonderful thing—bringing to life, to reality what skips around in one's imagination is another! How would it be possible to construct "the root of Jesse" in such a way that the breadth of this potent scriptural symbol could adequately meet the breadth and potency of our worship space? The search was on!

After the "Jesse tree" was mounted, only a few days before Advent was to break onto our horizon, I sat in the quiet of the church, giving thanks for the artistry and hard work of its creator and its "mounter" (the artist and the engineer!). Suddenly, in the midst of my admiration, I was overcome with *the power of the shadows*, now dramatically being cast by its roots, as they danced across the expanse of white wall. As the changing lights — both of the day and the electricity—interacted with the roots, the shadows began their dance. I was drawn into the subtle movements of the shadows, gently entering their dance steps, not unlike a shy teenager stepping into the embrace of his first date at a school party, and I became increasingly aware that these shadows, perhaps even more than the branches and roots of the tree itself, were a powerful signpost along the spiritual path of this Advent season. As the sun began to set, and the shadows grew more numerous and active, it was no longer the tree itself that mesmerized me, but now the shadows themselves, calling me into their Advent dance.

In our often too overly brilliant lights of the "Christmas" season (I think the Osborne's should take their lights back to Arkansas!), we miss the shadows. And yet, it seems to me, that there is much for us to learn while we dance with and among the shadows of Advent *before* we embrace the powerful Light of the Nations at Christmas. As Jan Richardson tells us in *Night Visions: Searching the Shadows of Advent and Christmas*, "But the sacred presence is there, breathing in the shadows. I believe that this is the gift that God holds out to us in this season: to carry the light, yes, but also to see in the dark and to find the shape of things in the shadows…."

We are moving toward the celebration of light, the Light of the World, the Light first announced by the brilliant Nativity Star, which guided the Magi to the Christ-child, but first we must spend time with the shadows of this season. To do so, however, may first stir our fears.

The "shadows" in our own lives—those of our personal choices and decision, those in our families and workplace, those that are cast within our nation, our church, and our world—like those that dance before us on the wall of our sanctuary, may seem larger than life, out of proportion. In this way, they may cripple us, overwhelm us. "Shadows" strike us as sneaky, deceptive, lurking, always trying to frighten us with unwelcome surprises. We sense that to "be in the shadows" means to be "out of the open," perhaps carrying on business that we should not be engaged in, or at least, business we don't want others to know about. Often, the shadows are where we lurk when we are ashamed of who we are or what we have done. Yes, to enter the Advent dance with the shadows can be frightening.

And yet, if the sacred presence is "breathing in the shadows," and if the shadows are indeed "God's gift" held out to us in this season, then we must move beyond our fears and shame and allow the beauty of the shadows to speak to us, to guide us, to prepare us for what lies ahead at the dawn of Christmas morning.

As the large and wild branches of the "Jesse tree" hang upon the wall, their shadows create an even larger, more expansive, richer and deeper symbol than the tree alone can provide. The shadows allow the tree to be more fully expressive and to reach out and in further than before. The shadows bring the now barren tree to life in a way, turning the somewhat static image into a symbol with movement. In the shadows, mystery is born; the hidden dimensions of life and of God can be embraced. There are always pieces of our lives and of God we don't see—even pieces that can be lost in the brightness of day.

Our invitation is to enter the Advent dance of the shadows—to explore those hidden, perhaps feared and fearful aspects of our lives, of our relationships with others, with our world, with our God. Take time in these often brilliantly lit days and nights to embrace the shadows dancing behind the glitz and glitter. Beware of "dressing up" the darkness, the emptiness, the shadows too much or too prematurely. This is the time for us to explore why it is and for what reasons we *need* Christ to come—what we want Christ to bring about, to heal, to embolden.

As Jack Boozer so eloquently says, "In this strange season when we are suspended between realization and expectation, may we be found *honest about the darkness.*" If we are honest about the darkness, about the shadows, perhaps then we will be more fully perceptive of the Light when He comes!

# "OH, FOR AN HOUR OF 'EMPTINESS' IN THIS SEASON OF FULLNESS!"

Sometimes there's a high price to pay for being a "neat freak." I suppose most people don't have a problem with letting things just pile up around the office or house, but some of us do. This past Sunday, December $6^{th}$, I awoke with a mild case of disappointment—I had *missed* the Feast of St. Nicholas! Actually, I didn't miss the "feast"; I missed setting out my *shoe* on Saturday night! If only I were the type of person who randomly dropped clothes and shoes around the house, I could have been spared the disappointment. If only I were a bit messier, I would have awoken to a sneaker or loafer filled with goodies (funny how we don't mind eating *food* out of an old shoe this one day a year!)

As I trod off to Mass that morning, I chastised myself for being so childish and for being a little greedy. Although I had given up on this missed opportunity, as it turned out, St. Nick was still to make an appearance—not by way of "shoe delivery," but in the guise of a friend.

I tried not to appear too enthusiastic, or too grabby, when I received my first Christmas present of the season! Despite it being the Feast of St. Nicholas, I silently reminded myself that after all, this is *Advent*, and we're supposed to be waiting, wondering, pacing ourselves; we're trying to distance ourselves, even if only so slightly, from the overkill of the consumer culture around us—the one that wants us to stand in line for hours (even days) for nonsensical stuffed toys that we've been brainwashed into purchasing!

I graciously thanked my friend for being so kind in getting a head start on the gift exchanging, and it was wonderful to receive a little lift in the midst of an extremely hectic time of year. The package was small, but brilliantly covered in that shiny-not-from-the-Dollar-Store kind of Christmas paper. My little treasure was even put together in what I like to call "soap opera gift packaging." Let me explain. If you've ever watched a soap opera (don't be afraid to admit it!), you'll notice that whenever someone receives a gift, especially at Christmas, he or she never has to *tear* any wrapping paper or wage war against never-say-die strapping tape in order to open the gift box. One simply lifts the lid off—neatly and cleanly. Soap opera characters seem to have plenty of room for "mess" in their personal lives, but *not* when it comes to gift exchanges!

Once out of sight of the gift giver, I gave my box a gentle shake; I'm a firm believer that good things *do* come in small packages. Shake…shake…shake…. Nothing!

Not a sound! I was bothered only momentarily, as my thoughts quickly turned to the possibility that a "silent" present might be buried within—the kind of present I could spend! That's the beauty of cash—never makes a sound!

Carefully I lifted the lid...and to my surprise...there was nothing inside! EMPTY! Oops! Maybe in the excitement of preparing this little token of seasonal joy, my friend had forgotten the contents!

Well, actually there *was* something inside—a note. The opening line read: "Over the next 19 days, may you be filled in many ways from this magical yet sacred gift of *emptiness.*" In an instant, my heart began to race and tears filled my eyes. This is exactly what I wanted, exactly what I needed—the gift of EMPTINESS. What a wonderfully gracious, generous gift!

In the days preceding the "Feast," I had been struggling with the glut of the season, with the overload and indulgence. I had been staring bleary-eyed at my calendar, contemplating all the events and commitments, all the formalities and festivities that were to fill nearly every minute of my days and nights in the weeks to come. In the quieter, less insane moments given to prayer (not that there had been much time for this either), I longed for a meaningful, purposeful experience of EMPTINESS. I pleaded with God for just an hour or two of emptiness to well up somewhere within the overdrive course I had been charting for myself.

Perhaps this prayerful supplication seems a bit odd. Don't we normally seem to revel in the "largeness" of this season? If this were not the case, why do people flock in droves (and they're not just tourists) to see 10 gazillion lights at Disney (personally, I wish the people of Arkansas would have been able to appreciate them enough so they could have stayed there!)? Why do we purchase so many gifts? Why do we bake more than one kind of cookie? Why isn't just one animated figure enough on our Christmas lawnscape? Christmas is BIG, BIG, BIG! Sure it may have started off small, but that was then, and this is now!

Perhaps this prayerful supplication seems a bit odd given the fact that this season, more than any other time of year, finds people struggling with depression, with sadness, with precisely what I had been asking for—EMPTINESS! Why would anyone want to seek from God the very thing that most of us spend our lives trying to avoid or deny? Isn't emptiness a scourge of human life that we struggle to drive away?

The kind of emptiness I have been seeking is not the down-in-the-dumps doldrums, the woe-is-me head hanging, the life-is-meaningless or Christmas-is-irredeemably-corrupt lament. It's not the emptiness of disappointment, or loneliness, or depression, or rejection. **It is, however, the emptiness of that hollow space where I have enough room to be receptive to God's desire and vision of who I am and where I am going.** It is creating emptiness within my heart-cradle, where Christ can be born and borne, where Jesus can find a resting place. In the midst of all the rush and rancor of this season of indulgence and fullness, I long for an emptiness that liberates me from the "cost" of striving to be filled. I don't want to be just another person in a long line of preoccupied inn-keepers who "have no room" for the Christ when he comes seeking a place to be born.

Is it possible for such emptiness? Is it merely a dream to be dashed once again by powers that seem much stronger, much more resourceful than I can wage battle with? Does it mean having to reject all that surrounds me? Does such emptiness require that I disconnect from everything and everyone within reach? Is this kind of emptiness possible?

As I contemplate this seemingly impossible task, the reassuring words of the angel spoken to Mary at the Annunciation slowly begin to chime repeatedly like the subtle tones of an old mantle clock—*nothing is impossible with God!* Faintly, like the lonely candles of the Advent wreath, a light begins to shine and to illuminate a path. I begin to see that emptiness is indeed present and available within the very things that are occupying my time and attention; all I need do is pause long enough to embrace the emptiness. All I need to do is see the emptiness as an *invitation* rather than scourge, to embrace it as friend rather than enemy. I begin to see it happening in small but significant ways.

It is possible to confront the emptiness of the barren

Christmas tree about to be loaded with color and lights. Once released from its plastic, mesh straightjacket, spend time gazing upon its simplicity, its beauty, as it stands tall in its place. Take in the empty, yet outstretched branches, silently calling for something to nest on its limbs.

It is possible to confront the emptiness of the Christmas Gift List still waiting to be completed with the "perfect" gift. Rather than being filled with stress and anxiety over the fact that the cherished item is no longer available, or was recently destroyed during the last "blue light special" surge of shoppers, it is possible to gaze long and hard at the emptiness of that space and to consider the "necessity" of the gift.

Is it possible to revel in the emptiness of the blank space on a Christmas card waiting to be filled with some personal greeting from "your house to theirs"? Rather than dashing off a quick "miss you," or "maybe see you next year," is it possible, through the gift of imagination, to linger over each person, each relationship, the joy of having known, as well as the pain of separation from her or him?

Is it possible to allow the emptiness of the church's décor, the starkness of the Advent environment to penetrate us, even as we contemplate what it will look like at Midnight Mass? Rather than trying to soften the harshness of the Advent landscape, perhaps brushing up next to its simplicity will be just irritating enough to stir up thoughts of honesty, purity, and the beauty present when all facades are stripped away.

Is it possible to gaze into the empty boxes, soon to be filled with Christmas presents, and to spend a moment or two contemplating the *real* gift behind the gift—if any? Before stuffing and cramming, before wrapping and pasting, is it possible to stare into the emptiness of the boxes and wonder what is it that I am really trying to give this person? Is what I am about to place in this package truly a meaningful sign of our relationship, truly an expression of who we are for each other?

In these and so many other ways, EMPTINESS knocks at my door, while I'm busy, distracting myself with other sounds. Yet I know all too well, there will be "no room at the inn" for Christ (or anyone else for that matter) unless first I answer the knock, and allow the EMPTINESS to make a home under my roof.

# ALUMINUM FOIL FOR THE WINDOWS?

I remember the first time I walked into a college student's room and took note of what I considered the peculiar décor on the windows. Temporarily distracted by the dirty laundry gathered in sizeable mounds around the floor, as well as the hefty number of beer bottles overflowing his tiny garbage pail, I soon returned to the windows, and wondered why they were covered with aluminum foil!

Never doubting the creativity of a dorm resident when it came to "making a home" for himself in a cramped, spartan cubicle, built for earlier generations of collegians who arrived at school with little more than a toothbrush and a radio, I imagined the aluminum foil was intended to produce some kind of greenhouse effect in the room.

Finally, unable to sit much longer with this unresolved mystery, I inquired about the foil. The answer came back quickly… "It's to keep the light out!" Not missing a beat, I shot back, "Well, that's obvious! It's 10 o'clock in the morning, but it seems like midnight in here! Why no light?"

Spoken like a true man-about-campus, the resident answered, "I like it dark; makes it easier to sleep late in the mornings." This made perfect sense to me realizing that college students are generally nocturnal in their lifestyles, and usually are vampire-esque in their disdain for early morning sunlight and 8am classes!

As we enter gently into this Season of Advent, when the shadows of the night grow longer and the hours of sunlight are diminished, I wonder where each of us stands in relationship to the Light? No, not the light of the sun streaming through windows nor the flicker of candles or bulbs, but rather the Light of Christ, which we anticipate again in these sacred days about to unfold.

It may seem like a strange thing to say, but at times, I believe that we, much like the student in the foil-wrapped dorm room, are afraid of the Light…but for different reasons other than sleeping in and cutting classes. Perhaps we know all too well that Light exposes, reveals, and brings out from hiding. As the First Letter to the Corinthians puts it, when the Lord Jesus comes, he will *bring to light the things now hidden in darkness and will disclose the purposes of the heart (4:5).* Given the secrets and unresolved movements we harbor there, would that we might wrap some aluminum foil around our souls in order to keep the purposes of our minds and hearts undisclosed and hidden in darkness. Sometimes the Light reveals more than we care to see for ourselves, let alone what others may discover.

Amidst the frenzy that has already been unleashed, the

one that our "economy" is so desperate to see split at the seams with spending power, our ability to leave behind the distracting "lights" of the season and to allow the true Light to penetrate us is somewhat compromised. It is a blessing, then, that Advent begins not with a blaze of luminescence, but rather with one lonely candle casting its fragile flame toward us. Allowing the Light to enter into the protective crevices of our souls, to truly shine in the places where real decisions and choices are being made for living, must be a gradual thing, an incremental process—one candle at a time. Like the prisoner, bolted behind the steel door of solitary confinement for weeks on end, whose eyes cannot accept a sudden burst of light, we too become accustomed to the darkness, to those hidden ways of living—some of which we are not proud—our infidelities, our complacency and resignations, our poor-me-ism and self-loathing, our jealousy and envy, our cheating and stealing, our prejudice and bigotry. These shadows prefer to stay where they are, to be sealed with "foil" against the Light, yet we know in faith that the Light cannot be deterred; the Light comes and cannot be extinguished!

*This light is now entrusted to you to be kept burning brightly... for you must always walk as a child of the light!* The joyous words spoken on the day of baptism, when yet another fragile, flickering flame was handed either to us or to our godparents, remind us of who we are and to what we are called. Thus, as we are invited to enter into this sacred Advent of our God, let us take to heart the words of the

Letter to the Ephesians:

*For once you were in darkness, but now in the Lord you are light. Live as children of light—for the fruit of the light is found in all that is good and right and true. Try to find out what is pleasing to the Lord. Take no part in the unfruitful works of darkness, but instead expose them…. Everything exposed by the light becomes visible, for everything that becomes visible is light. Therefore it says, 'Sleeper, awake! Rise from the dead, and Christ will shine on you.'*

Plato, the great Greek philosopher, once wrote: *We can easily forgive a child who is afraid of the dark; the real tragedy is when men are afraid of the light.*

As we "sleepers" heed the call to awaken these Advent days, let us gradually enter into the Light, gradually allow the Light to illumine our minds and hearts, so that when Christmas dawns, we may find more than presents unwrapped. May *we* have the courage to be "unwrapped" from the protective covers we place around ourselves, and truly shine with the Light of Christ!

# TALLYING UP THE *PROPHETS* (NOT PROFITS) OF THE SEASON

Well...in the eyes, hearts and balance sheets of the retail and e-tail worlds...it's all over! Whew! It's been a long season (just ask my sister, who has spent much of her working life in retail management)! Sure, there'll be a few attempts made to bolster the numbers with after-holiday clearances and other voodoo-economic tabulations to make the season a couple of stomach-turns less than nauseating for corporate honchos and stock holders. We've been reading about it for weeks...and there will still be a few more to come—pronouncing the final "profit-cies" for another Christmas.

But I'm looking to the ***prophets***, not the profits, for a real test of whether this Advent-Christmas season has had an anemic effect on the bottom line of the disciples of Christ, or whether it has jolted us into deeper commitment toward peace, justice, wonder, awe, courage in the face of the culture of death, compassion for the poor, understanding and empathy for today's wandering nomads in search of a safe harbor, and true "holy communion" in the family of God.

If we were taking heed, the Advent-Christmas journey *exposed* us (just as radically as the fabled "emperor with no clothes") to the power of the real prophets and their ability to literally change the course of direction of not only our own souls, and those of all peoples, but even the course of the cosmos. While some may imagine that dollars-and-cents profits are the only means to either lift up people from the pit, or to knock them down from their lofty, comfy, gated thrones, those of us who take seriously the living Word of God, and the presence of the Kingdom of God know that prophets are the ones whose message either opens the opportunity to live in the light of the deepest desires God has for God's creation, or casts out the foolish where there will be wailing and grinding of teeth.

The profits of Christmas have not been without their blessings: nice new things, a few more toys to enjoy; perhaps a much-needed appliance or step-saver for the home or office; even a good bit of legitimate and generous sharing with those whose experience of profits lifting them up is far less than even "sugar plums dancing in their heads."

But the profits of Christmas have also, once again, wreaked havoc in our lives: disappointing Christmas mornings filled with less than we had expected; influxes of goods that we'll never be able to keep up with; consumer debt that buries us for months and months to come; guilt for not being able to give what we hoped to give to others; perhaps despair that we got caught up in the madness to begin with; as well as both exhaustion and a sigh of relief that "Christmas is over".

But I'm looking to see what the *prophets* have wrought this Advent-Christmas season. Who will give an assessment of their impact on the people of God? How can we count or number their influence; their power to straighten out our crooked ways; the tools they provided us for mountain-leveling and valley-filling; their audacity to lead us to believe that wolf and lamb, leopard and kid, calf and young lion shall browse together, and that implements of war can be turned into implements of food and life; and their blatant acceptance that "imagination" is more powerful than any calculus or political agenda?

How will we measure these *prophets* and the way they have shaped us this Advent-Christmas? Only you and I can give an accounting for this. Or perhaps more accurately, those around us will give an accounting of the changes, the progress, the renewal these prophets have brought us who claim that Jesus Christ is the Son of God, Savior of the world, Emmanuel—because they will either see changed lives, renewed spirits, softened hearts, committed witness—or they will not!

Surely, we'll wade our way through the "mixed signals" being sent by the profits that will be massaged every which way as Christmas comes to a close. But the accounting we are asked to give, the bottom line on the balance sheet of this Advent-Christmas season will get no press in the media—they will have already forgotten all the light of goodness and generosity that was able to flow from the hearts and wallets of kind, caring, and justice-striving people—and will once again turn our attention to the darkness that still veils much of our world (especially as politics most likely will become more heated, more ugly, and more disgraceful in the months to come).

I suppose, this year, there's one advantage of our Lenten journey following up so quickly on the heels of this holy and gracious season of celebrating the Incarnation of the Son of God—we'll get another six weeks to try again, as the great mystic Meister Eckhart wrote so profoundly centuries ago, ***to be mothers of God...to give birth to him in my time and my culture. This then is the fullness of time: when the Son of God is begotten in us."***

Does anyone want to give an accounting, to tally up the impact the real *prophets* have had over these past weeks? Are we thankful that "Christmas is over," or will we continue to hear the prophets' clarion call in every season?

# MAKING A LIST, CHECKING IT TWICE... TO SEE WHAT I ALREADY POSSESS

I'm not sure what kids are doing ever since Sears did away with their giant Christmas catalog! During the days of my childhood, long before any department store Santa mounted his throne in preparation to receive chatty children on his knees, every child I knew turned to the greatest reference book on the face of the earth for pre-Christmas "Santa Wish Lists" (I say "reference" because I'm sure I rarely ever received anything directly from this catalog). I recall meticulously pouring over each page in the massive toy section like an archeologist in search of a priceless relic buried in the ancient desert sands. With more intensity that I could ever muster for a whole year's worth of homework assignments, I joyfully focused on this most necessary of "homework" assignments, searching every picture and descriptive text with rapture. No detail of those pages escaped me—except, of course, the *prices* that were listed next to the items (I presumed Santa, given his unlimited beneficence, coupled with my stellar behavior in the weeks prior to Christmas, could hardly be concerned about such silly things as prices). With great pride, I would present my extensive list, now fully prepared after days and nights of hard labor, to my parents for their initial perusal. I counted on them to give the final seal of approval for the quality of my spelling, grammar, and penmanship. Although I do not recall the elaborate intricacies of their arguments, or the sophisticated logic that must have been employed, I do undoubtedly recall my mom and dad convincing me to *considerably* pare down that "Wish List." Whatever methods they employed, they must have worked, since I never had to put extra postage on the envelope of my "Letter to Santa"!

There may not be a Sears Wish Book for Christmas, but each of us finds a way to take stock of our possessions and to create our "Wish List" for the "Santa" in our lives. Even when we try to hold back and take a more simple approach to the season of gift-giving and receiving, we have to contend with some friend or family member breathing down our neck reminding us, "how hard we are to buy for," and we had better get our act together! Some are so aggressive that no sooner than the hot dogs and baked beans from our Labor Day cookout get cold, they start harping on us about Christmas being "just around the corner" and that NOW is the time to figure out what we WANT!

Usually, the easiest place to begin piecing together our gift-request list is to take account of what we already possess. We scan the rows of clothes in our closets; we tumble through our dresser and desk drawers; we scour our tool shed, craft or sewing room; we pry into every nook and cranny of the kitchen or attic; we count the number of televisions, stereos, DVD and CD players, or other electronic gadgetry we own; we inventory our stock-pile of games and toys (grown-up and children); we survey every curio cabinet, countertop, and bric-a-brac shelf in the house. Then...having plowed through the mountains of what we already possess, we use our imaginations to add on even more!

But there is something strange about this process. Instead of recognizing what we do possess, and giving thanks for it, we rather focus on what we do not yet have! Having been exhausted by our investigations, we focus on what is still lacking amongst our many possessions, and we seek to rectify those shortcomings by proffering our "Wish Lists" to family and friends.

In the desire (or pressure) to come up with things we "need" or "want," we often can only see what is lacking rather than what we do possess. I say this not to create another layer of guilt about the enormity of our material wealth, but to give us pause for thankfulness. In this season of taking account of our belongings (*both* material and spiritual), when we focus on what we are missing and still desire to possess, let us bask in the gifts already received, the generosities already lavished upon us, the beauty of treasures already shared, the graciousness of gifts already received.

Looking around the crowded space of my life, both without and within, I'll bet I can put together a "THANK YOU LIST" whose length and breadth would rival or surpass any childhood "Wish List" that made its way to Santa's North Pole!

# CHRISTMAS

*Think about all the "unusual and extraordinary" things we do at this time of year that, for the most part, would be deemed unreasonable and strange if they occurred at any other time. Sometimes, in a struggling attempt to explain ourselves, we stutteringly say: "Well...it's...it's...it's Christmas!" And in saying that word, "Christmas," everything is made all right; everything becomes understandable.*
*While we wistfully ponder the possibility of the kind of world where it would be "Christmas all year," while we wonder at the ability of humankind to make the "unusual" and "extraordinary" more a regular pattern of our living, we also wake each day, as people of faith, knowing that God's promises to us have been fulfilled. Emmanuel, God-With-Us is no helpless baby lying in a manger, but rather the Great God who comes to save, the "Wonder-Counselor, God-Hero, Father-Forever, and Prince of Peace".*

# FINDING GOD IN THE "WRONG PLACES"

It was to be my last full day in Boston before making the move back to Chicago. I was finishing up my doctoral studies and preparing to bid farewell to a wonderful parish community, who had graciously provided a warm home for me during my studies. St. Angela's parish, nestled in the tough and impoverished Mattapan neighborhood, despite its economic struggles, had a big enough heart to make room for a student-priest and blessed me with many experiences of Christ's multi-cultural presence.

Although I had been living in Boston for over a year and had tried to make the most of my abbreviated respites from my academic work at Boston University, I had not been able to travel to Cape Cod, nor to Plymouth Rock. Somehow, I thought that in the days and years to come, as I unfolded the memories of my stay in New England, I would be forever embarrassed to admit that I had never ventured to these "sacred" sites!

Fortunately, some good people who had befriended

me during my time at St. Angela's, welcoming me into their home, especially for the holidays that passed in those months, saved me from this future infamy by planning a surprise trek down the coast to Plymouth and then on to the Cape. Days before the adventure, I was simply told to be ready for one final day-trip as a parting gift from them to me. (I learned later that they had overheard my lament about missing out on these two tourist "must-sees".)

While the Cape is every bit as rustic, romantic, picturesque, quaint and quirky as the brochures so eloquently describe, it is the trip to Plymouth Rock that jogs my memory now. In a word…it was a…DUMP!

As we made our way to Plymouth, passing all the glowing signs indicating our proximity to this bastion of American freedom and glory, I could feel the excitement building in me. Visions of Thanksgiving plays at school, people dressed in heavy clothes and sporting those comical buckled shoes, childhood songs about the Pilgrims and their precarious landing in the "new world"—all sprung to life with richness and vibrancy.

And then we arrived…parked the car…made our way to the water's edge and the always recognizable historical marker post—and saw the famous "ROCK!" What a major disappointment! It really wasn't much of a "rock" at all. In fact, my parents have removed far larger ones from their backyard in the mountains of Pennsylvania than the one that anchored the Pilgrims upon their arrival. Not only was it puny, but also it was surrounded by a dilapidated fence (must have been erected not long after the first Pilgrims toed the shoreline!) that seemed only to serve the purpose of corralling all the garbage and trash people tossed away before leaving this historic site.

I came looking for something wonderful, impressive, magnificent, and stirring—but instead found something quite the opposite. If not for the historical marker, clearly setting out the data about this storied spot, I would have thought I was in the wrong place!

Plymouth Rock and the home in Bethlehem where the Magi eventually arrived are far removed from each other in time and place and significance—but the experience of my journey and that of the eastern sages has something in common. We both thought we had found the wrong place—because what we believed to be, wanted to be, hoped to be so spectacular and breath-taking, was wrapped as plainly as could be. For me, it was the historical marker alone that forced me to see I was not deceived by the sight…for the Magi it was the star alone that forced them to see they were not deceived in their search for the "newborn King of the Jews."

How often in the journeys of our lives, especially in our searching and seeking for God and God's presence, do we think we have come to the wrong place because it doesn't fit our preconceived notions and dreams about who God is and how God should make God's self known? We set out, much like the Magi, with plans and maps and "wisdom" that has been passed on to us, and we make our steps confident that in the end we will meet and know God. Along the way, we stumble and get lost, we lose heart, we wonder if the venture is worth the investment—but somehow we persevere because it is God whom we seek—and we believe God is worth the costs of the journey.

And then we "arrive"—at least we come to a place or experience that we believe is what God is supposed to be like—and we think we've been duped; we think we were misled by priests, and teachers, and scriptures, and ceremonies, and regulations. We come to discover a God who is so plainly wrapped that we wonder about all the fuss—all the stuff that makes up the path of our religious traditions. We come to discover a God who is so plainly dressed that we doubt there's anything special there.

A wafer of wheat, a sip of inexpensive wine, a gentle hand, a dab of oil on the forehead, a broken heart crying out for comfort, a weeping child, the smile of a spouse, the warmth of bodies entwined in love, a simple "thank you," a few moments spent on bended knees in the darkness, the splash of water in a baptismal font, the ache of loneliness, the rock-bottom of addiction, the sun rising or setting over the horizon, the laughter of aged bingo players in the nursing home, the flower gently placed upon the lowered casket, a photograph from a sweeter and more tender time in life—all so plain, so unnoticeable at first, so unpretentious and unassuming. Are these the places we must look for God? Are these the kinds of places where the shining star of Bethlehem is meant to lead all the "magi" who take up the journey in search of the Christ?

The wonder and mystery of the Incarnation seems to answer a wholehearted YES to those questions. A baby, with no credentials, was the endpoint of the Magi's long and arduous search—and yet, upon their arrival in what must have seemed like the wrong place—they knelt down in humility—a humility borne from looking in the "wrong place," for expecting something royally spectacular and impressive.

Let us also kneel in humility before the God who comes to us in ways beyond our imaginings, yet mostly in small and oh-so-easily missed times and places and encounters and people. Let us celebrate our plain-wrapper God who sneaks into our lives while we are busy looking elsewhere.

# "HEY, WE WERE HERE FIRST!"

I can almost hear the infamous shepherding clans who, in the middle of tending the night watch, were suddenly overwhelmed by a heavenly chorus and bizarre instructions to rush to a cave where a feeding trough was now cradling the long-awaited Savior of the world.

No, not hear them back then on that first wondrous Christmas night…but rather "hear" them now. I imagine the shepherds walking through a religious supply house or local Hallmark Superstore, fighting their way through Snoopy ornaments and Sno-Babies, and finally gazing upon the somewhat familiar territory of our modern Nativity crèche scenes, and in their loudest sheep-tending-chasing-corralling voices shouting: "What's the deal? **You left us out**—replaced by three guys, dressed to the nines in crowns and glittery robes, and a couple of camels! You think sheep smell? Well, wait until you get a whiff of those humped-back behemoths! We may not be the cleanest, prettiest, best-dressed folks on the hillside, **but have you forgotten—we were there first!** Just double-check with

Luke!" (They'd get an argument, however, from Matthew, who also leaves them out of the story. Then, of course, there's Mark who says nothing of the "birth" of Jesus, and John, well, he's floating through the cosmos when he gets on the Incarnation subject).

A funny thing seems to have happened on the way to the Nativity, at least as the makers of modern crèches (mostly from China—so watch out for the lead, folks!) deem fit to recreate the sacred event in their resin and ceramic figurines—the shepherds are disappearing!

While I've personally been a fan of the three (or more?) wise men over the years, and count our liturgical celebration of the Epiphany Feast as one of my most favorite of the Church calendar, I'm a little perplexed at the rapid decline in the presence of the shepherds. I suppose there is something much more glamorous and intriguing about the visitors from the East who come to pay homage to the Christ child, despite their apparent lack of a sense of direction and the consequent late arrival, than there is about the flock-tenders. Looking at most Nativity scenes for sale today, I suppose that if somebody has to go, the wise men are worth keeping: they cut a fine figure; fit our modern penchant for cultural and religious diversity; and make this otherwise humble and earthy birth chamber much more extravagant.

But the shepherds—that's another story! While the little lambs may be cute and cuddly, a nice touch to round out the menagerie of stable animals, the shepherds (men and women) tend to crowd the scene, so they are deemed expendable. Not that they're unavailable for purchase, but many crèches just skip the unattractive, less romantic people—a nice cost-cutting maneuver. Besides, how many people can you fit inside a musical Christmas snow globe anyway? Yet, as my imagined shepherds make clear to us—they are not expendable; in fact, they were there first, as described by the Evangelist Luke —and they are an integral facet in the diamond that is the Incarnation of the Son of God. After all, the newborn babe, as he grew into manhood, spent more of his time with the shepherd-types, i.e. the poor, dirty, struggling, outcast, off-color, scrappy, and forgotten folks, than he did with the regal, be-jeweled and attractive ones. Perhaps as Jesus heard about these rough-and-tumble first-night visitors, when the tales of his birth were recounted by Mary and Joseph years later, the seed of his future self identity as the "Good Shepherd" was planted deep into the ground of his soul.

In an essay written by Wynne S. Gillis entitled *The Truth About Shepherds,* the author colorfully describes the perplexing consequence of embracing the Nativity shepherds. Rewriting Luke 2:8 for a contemporary audience, Willis imagines: *And there were in the same country…a bunch of dirty, thieving nomads; there were street people, huddled over a heating grate by night, passing around cheap wine in a paper sack….* The shepherds of Luke's account and Jesus' day belonged to one of the most despised trades (perhaps only exceeded in annoyance and hatred by the tax collectors); the kind of people one avoided, if not for their conniving, pushy antics, then for their hygienic and un-kosher atrocities!

And yet, Willis reminds us that God avoided all the "upright, faithful Temple-goers" and chose to trumpet the Good News through a scraggly band of outcasts. *By choosing the outcasts of society, God declared there is no one beyond the bounds of his love. No one is too dirty, too sinful, too despised. There is no place too ugly for his presence, whether a sheep pasture or a cross.*

While the wise men have their own powerful and equally unsettling story to tell us, their own way of upsetting our "plans" for the way we think that God should come into our world, the shepherds cannot be ignored and are worth our contemplation in these glorious days of Christmastide.

Are there "shepherds" that I am ignoring, pushing to the margins, or simply telling to stay in their place or keep their distance from me? Am I perhaps a "shepherd," feeling too dirty, too sinful, or too lost-and-forgotten to even merit a "post-card" reminder that Jesus Christ is forever the light of the world, a light which no darkness can overcome?

Lest we forget…***in that region there were shepherds living in the fields, keeping watch over their flock by night. Then an angel of the Lord stood before them, and the glory of the Lord shone around them, and they were terrified. But the angel said to them, 'Do***

***not be afraid; for see—I am bringing you good news of great joy for all the people' (Luke 2:8-10 NRSV).***

The wise men will soon have their day, and will tell us their side of things, but for now—let us spend time on the "edges" this Christmas, and see how God *mostly still* chooses to come.

# WRAPPING THINGS UP FOR CHRISTMAS

There are many ways in which the world is divided; there are many ways in which people are divided—categorized, labeled, marked out. One such way of identifying people that strikes me at Christmas time is whether or not someone is a *believer in gift wrap* or a *disdainer of gift wrap*. Let me explain…

There seems to be a category of people who simply don't get all the fussing about gift wrapping. They reluctantly purchase great quantities of it from desperate school children (and their even more desperate parents) in order to support the children's elementary school; they openly laugh at people in the "paper and bow" aisle of the Walgreens trying to decide whether to go with the "Super Deluxe Jumbo" roll or the nifty little packages of gift wrap squares; they couldn't care less about not knowing how to tie a bow or how to cross ribbon properly around a package. You see, for this category of humanity, gift wrapping makes absolutely no sense—and shouldn't be so time-consuming or worrisome. After all, as they all-too-proudly profess…IT GETS TORN INTO PIECES IN A MATTER OF SECONDS! Why bother?

Those disdainers of Christmas gift wrapping see more purpose in dental flossing (such a rare breed, indeed) than in spending countless hours picking out one's favorite wrapping paper and bows, and then wrestling with scissors and tape and ribbon in order to make all the gifts look like they just leapt off the pages of a Christmas designer magazine. The whole thing just makes no sense whatsoever! For this breed of Christmas shopper, simply gathering up the comic pages of the newspaper from two weeks before Christmas would be festive enough to slap around the Christmas packages. For the dyed-in-the-wool disdainer, however, even this would be deemed excessive. Simply put it under the tree and say, "Merry Christmas!"

On the other hand, there are those of us who revel in bright and beautiful Christmas wrappings, hardly concerned that we could have bought a few more gifts (or perhaps significantly lowered the balance on our credit cards) if not for the extensive amount of wrapping bobbles and bangles we invested in this year! For those of us on this side of the wrapping paper hemisphere, Christmas gifts are made even more special, more "personal" by the wrapping with which we so painstakingly encircle them. We are the true artists, the ones who appreciate the aesthetics of the whole Christmas experience, from the shiny top of the Christmas tree to the glitter of the packages resting majestically below its branches.

We have little concern that someone is going to tear our packaging to shreds within moments of receiving the gift. It's the total "experience" we are going for. We liken our methodical art of Christmas packaging to the gourmet chef who, after slaving over a hot stove and oven to produce the masterpiece about to be eaten, still makes sure that the *appearance* of the food completes the experience. As most gourmands will tell you, "presentation" is everything!

As I wrapped my packages and received many beautiful ones this Christmas, I began thinking about the beauty of God's "packaging"—the way God arrays God's Creation with splendor and majesty. God makes a unique statement about each of us as we are "packaged" and come to life in this world.

However, God's packaging reveals a beauty that goes beyond glitz and glitter. In fact, some of God's most precious and most striking "wrapping" of humanity comes amidst the depths of poverty and want. Some of the most beautiful faces and the warmest hearts radiate from the *anawim, the poor ones* of God's Creation. While a small portion of the world primps and postures with extravagant potions and lotions, all in the hopes of looking beautiful, the majority of the world lives each day simply "wrapped and covered" in the natural beauty of God's handiwork.

As we stare into the manger scenes of our homes and churches this Christmas, we are also reminded that when receiving the gift of God's Son, this gift didn't come in fancy wrappings (despite the talk of angelic choruses and Christmas stars shining). Rather Jesus Christ came into this world "swaddled" in weakness, rejection (no room at the inn), fragility, and mortal humanity. Placed in the feed trough for animals, this Jesus, this Incarnate Word of the Father, would continue to "feed" all humanity for the life of the world.

I suppose, it is clear that God chooses the side of the world that cares little for fancy wrapping. Yet, perhaps there is room in the world for both the *believers* and the *disdainers*—for when I see the beauty of a wrapped Christmas gift, all aglow with bows and bangles, I am reminded that God's gifts are always given in beauty and love, shining forth for all to embrace!

# "WELL, SO THAT IS THAT!" THOUGHTS WHILE DISMANTLING CHRISTMAS

*In the words of the poet W.H. Auden,*
*"Well, so that is that!"*

Christmas is over, as if we needed any reminders. In fact, one might find it strange that I am just now coming to this realization or even reflecting upon this truth, after all, it's nearly three weeks since the blessed commemoration! Why Christmas has been over for quite some time, hasn't it? For the most Scrooge-like among us, it was over before it even began—which is another story—seeing that it "began" sometime between our last dip in the ocean's summer warmth and the carving of the jack-o-lanterns!

Some of my neighbors were much more efficient than me, seemingly dismantling Christmas within hours of the clock striking midnight on December 25. I, on the other hand, like many folks, have to squeeze household chores in between my work schedule (that's right, priests have homes to take care of, too, in between work hours). I was relieved, after a quick stroll around the block, to find that other "inefficient" neighbors like me still were lighting their lawns right through Epiphany—either because they are extremely devout Christians, or because everything was still connected to their porch light switch, so they had no choice but to recharge their Christmas displays each night, at least until they also could dismantle Christmas. I must admit, though, after New Year's Day, my outdoor lights remained dark. Had nothing to do with turning pagan, nor forgetting about the celebration of the Wise Men, nor having had my fill of Christmas festivity—no, the decision to cancel the nightly illuminations was quite pragmatic—had more to do with the electric bill—since our lengthy deep chill necessitated running the furnace at a constant clip for over a week and a half!

As I engaged in the tedious and depressing process of dismantling Christmas, carefully packing away all the decorations, frightfully wondering if they, as the scriptures say, "were fruitful and multiplied" during their holiday run, since I now can't seem to be able to fit them into their original storage boxes I pulled down from the attic! (Probably doesn't help any that I am always a fool for a good, healthy After-Christmas Clearance Sale—adding to my decorative repertoire each year). The house always seems so glum and barren after everything is stowed away, less festive and colorful. I secretly ponder if it's really dull all year around, and I simply get accustomed to it!?

After the last box is lifted into the attic, and I have successfully navigated another year of not falling through the rafters or poking my arm through the air conditioning ductwork, I'm often given to reflection. Mind you, it's an uneasy kind of reflectiveness—the kind we often want to stay clear of—because it's the kind of soul-searching that makes one stop and sheepishly inquire—**what has this all been about?** Is it really possible to treat Christmas like we do so many other "tasks" undertaken in our lives? Once we have muddled through our obligations, put the finishing touches on the commitments and celebrations, unwrapped the last package, forced down the last sugar cookie, which by now has lost its sprinkles, moved the furniture back and cleaned up the hot chocolate stains and pine needles, and disposed of the child's shirt in which the candy cane melted in the pocket during the dryer's fluff cycle—is there nothing else we can do but sit back and declare: "**Well, so that is that!**"**?**

In my post-Christmas efforts to help the sagging retail economy from its incessant grieving and mourning, I sped off to the bookstore to cash in some of my most appreciated and treasured Christmas gifts—debit cards for purchasing books and other literary trinkets. While perusing the almost barren "Christmas shelf" at Borders (very quickly, though, since nothing was marked down—after Christmas, a true shopper simply bypasses any tables or racks not announcing "drastic markdowns"), I came upon an anthology of Christmas literary gems. As I skimmed the pages, I was immediately struck by a poem buried near the end of the volume, written by W.H. Auden.

The Oxford-educated British poet, as I recalled from my literature studies, lived in times when industrial stagnation and cultural decline were threatening England because of economic depression. He, like many of the poets of his age, wrestled with the complexities of modern societies' ills. Auden, therefore, is always one to raise the difficult, irritating questions in his poetry. The opening line of this poem struck a chord and promptly fueled several days of meditating on what had transpired over the Christmas holidays. All the while, I kept hearing those chilling words, "Well, so that is that"—and wrestling with whether or not I have been simply dusting the glitter from my hands and pulling pins out of crisp new shirts—believing and acting in ways that reveal the same sentiments: "so that is that!" And now…it is simply on to the next event, the next commitment, the next program or ministerial expectation, the next liturgical season.

Here are W.H. Auden's unnerving words in full:

"WELL, SO THAT IS THAT!" THOUGHTS WHILE DISMANTLING CHRISTMAS

*Well, so that is that. Now we must dismantle the tree,*
*Putting the decorations back into their cardboard boxes—*
*Some have got broken—and carrying them up to the attic.*
*The holly and the mistletoe must be taken down and burnt,*
*And the children got ready for school. There are enough*
*Left-overs to do, warmed up, for the rest of the week—*
*Not that we have much appetite, having drunk such a lot,*
*Staying up so late, attempted—quite unsuccessfully—*
*To love all our relatives, and in general*
*Grossly overestimated our powers. Once again*
*As in previous years we have seen the actual Vision and failed*
*To do more than entertain it as an agreeable*
*Possibility, once again we have sent Him away*
*Begging though to remain His disobedient servant,*
*The promising child who cannot keep His word for long.*

*(W.H. Auden, from "The Flight Into Egypt," Collected poems, ed. Edward Mendelson, 1944, 1972)*

I know that I am uncomfortable standing up against the accusations that *once again as in previous years we have seen the actual Vision and failed to more than entertain it as an agreeable possibility*.... Is the "Vision" of God, what the prophets in every age proclaim, and what God gives birth to in Jesus the Christ, nothing more than an "agreeable possibility"? Is all the fanfare, festivity and celebration; the moving prayer and worship in which we have participated; the promises and blessings offered; the triumphant procession of the Magi; the tender letters received in wondrous Christmas cards; the beautiful and touching gifts offered and received, unwrapped in the presence of loved ones, trying to express their deep and abiding care for us; the soft renditions of *Silent Night* sending shivers down our spine; and the bouncing orchestral shouts of *Joy to the World*—are all these, and so much more that defines our Christmases, only an attempt to "pretend," to play at the Vision? Or perhaps, do these expressions actually shield us from the TRUTH of the Vision, the truth of our faith, which is conveniently pushed aside at Christmas, only to come rushing back full force during Lent-Easter: that the Son of God must first be rejected, suffer and die—and then raised up by God?

In my own struggle in faith, I desperately want Christmas to be more than a set of tasks—no matter how troublesome or joyous—that I simply breathe a sigh of relief when they are over and then utter a plaintive "well, so that is that." Along with many others, I'm sure I put a lot of pressure on the Christmas season, expecting it to be so large and wondrous that the "Vision" is fortified for the remainder of the year, built up and strengthened enough that it's available when the doubts and frustrations rear their ugly heads. Yet, I keep finding, more and more as the years go by, that as "large" as we make Christmas, it's not enough to sustain the "Vision" that God has for us—it's only the beginning, albeit an important beginning. As I contemplate Christmas as something much "smaller" than we have made it into, I slowly begin to see why the early centuries of Christianity paid little attention to the "birth" of Christ, why they were not concerned about mangers and shepherds, wise ones and shining stars. For our early forbearers in faith, Christmas was "small," a beginning like any other birth. They were more concerned about what happened to the baby when he became a man and radically changed the course of life for anyone who would dare be his follower.

Somehow, we need to put less pressure on Christmas... or perhaps it is better to say, put less pressure *on ourselves at Christmas.* Christmas rekindles the joy and hope of God's Vision for humanity and all creation, but it cannot sustain it. No, it is what happens between Christmas and the Ascension that really tells the story, the whole story, and what emboldens us to live our lives each day with some measure of grace and purpose.

It is easy, particularly with pressures that come from all around us, to simply pack the boxes away and forget about climbing on the roof for another year, and to joyfully say, "Well, that is that!" But at least, when I am tempted to say it, or have in fact said it in exasperation, I know that I have been *reluctant* to say it—and down deep, I know I don't mean it; I don't really want it to go away.

But we must move on, venture further, move more deeply into "The Story" of the One who was born in Bethlehem obscurity, the One who grows into a man, a man who becomes the source of the "rise and fall of many." Christmas is over…but its promises and hopes, its challenges and upsetting agenda, its demands and consequences *are not over*, not packed away, not sealed with strapping tape and placed in the attic. Not *"that* is NOT that," for the Vision must be ever made new, must ever be recommitted to with zeal and passion, must not be forgotten like "days of Auld Lang Syne."

The grand Vision of God, proclaimed in God's Word, celebrated at God's table, and rooted in human hearts, is not "an agreeable possibility." In fact, for much of the world and its ways, even for ourselves at times, it is rather a quite *disagreeable* REALITY, for the Kingdom of God, Jesus' great Vision and revelation to humanity, is already among us; is already changing lives and undoing injustices; is already comforting the sick and afflicted; is already walking hand-in-heart with those who grieve and mourn; is already setting captives free and bringing light into the corners of intense darkness. No, this Vision must not be entertained as an "agreeable possibility," but rather must be pursued by women and men and children of faith as an ABIDING REALITY, one that has already been witnessed in our lives and must now be proclaimed to anyone within hearing distance!

Yes, the "end" of Christmas is depressing; yes, I've probably expected too much out of lights and presents and people; yes, I've put a lot of pressure on myself and Christmas to be the all-sustaining power for a "good year"—and unfortunately, I am quite susceptible to repeating these mistakes come Christmas next year! But, in grappling with the dilemma of "well, so that is that," I have come once again to gather up what I can from the joys and festivities of Christmas, especially the deeply touching gestures of love and care which I received in abundance, and now *to see beyond Christmas*, and to return to the work of being in partnership with God and God's people as we usher in the Vision through God's grace and favor.

Dismantling Christmas is *not* dismantling what it is all about. Yes, the tree is down, the wrappings burnt, the cookies eaten, the lights untangled, the house and church returned to their somewhat ordinary dullness—but *Christmas* goes on and on every day that disciples of Christ, men and women and children of faith keep the Vision alive and operative in their minds, hands and hearts, and manifest it to those whom they meet.

# LENT

*Caroline Adams once wrote: "Your life is like a sacred journey. You are on the path...exactly where you are meant to be right now...and from here, you can only go forward." In these Lenten days that are breaking open, we continue on our sacred journey, but it is, as all journeys must be, undertaken one step at a time! This Lenten journey runs the risk of being lost to us and devoid of any value, meaning, or purpose unless we commit ourselves to journey this sacred path one step at a time. There is danger in making too many plans, offering too many sacrifices, laying out a "program" too far in advance. We'll never digest a Lent we try to swallow all at once! No, these days are too sacred, far too life-altering to simply charge into them in a spiritual frenzy. This sacred 40-day path must be entered quietly, gently, and with a conviction that this Lent will be like no other we have experienced in our lives.*

# SITTING IN ASHES:
## *OUR LENTEN POSTURE*

During my college campus ministry days, Ash Wednesday used to drive me crazy. In spite of the fact that we held several liturgies throughout the day, with the distribution of ashes taking place at each of them, they never seemed to be sufficient—mind you, not as far as I was concerned. People wanted ashes—that's all there was to it. In fact, it became somewhat of a circus, as people kept coming to the Student Life office every few minutes throughout the entire day, sheepishly looking for "ashes-on- demand"! No sooner would my partner and I finish washing up from the last application of ashes, when in would walk another desperate Catholic, teetering on what they thought was the precipice of mortal sin! After all, they queried, isn't today a "holy day of obligation"?

My last year at the college, perhaps feeling the boldness and courage that only seems to come with one's impending departure from a job, I decided to either end the circus, or perhaps to make it even grander (depending on one's viewpoint). Lest I be severely criticized for denying someone the opportunity to celebrate their faith, or for turning off yet another soul to the Church, or simply being another inhospitable priest, I placed a large bowl of ashes in our office—with a quickly-drawn sign that read, in heavy, inviting-sized letters: "HELP YOURSELF!" But...beneath these...I scripted, ever so slightly (the kind of microscopic printing reserved for "guarantees" and "Publisher's Clearing House" Contest Rules): "Beware! Once they are on...they're hard to get off!"

ASHES are not objects in a religious game...or a blessing...nor a pious amulet or good luck charm...nor a "badge" of Catholicism (even "Protestants" use ashes now). They're neither a "club" emblem nor a safety seal.

ASHES are a STAIN... something DIRTY... something UNSETTLING. Ashes are hard to get rid of; ashes are hard to clean up, to wipe away.

Although the liturgical rubrics for Ash Wednesday liturgy indicate that "after the giving of ashes the priest and other ministers wash their hands , in reality, they'll never come off completely, whether from the fingertips of the ministers or from the foreheads of the faithful! Ashes are hard to be rid of. Ashes are all around us.

The ashes we wear do not STAIN us for a moment... or a day...or a "season". Rather, they SOIL us in every moment, in every day, in the course of every season. Ashes are all around us, but we usually don't want to see them. We want to wipe them away—quickly, efficiently, permanently. We may abide with them for a day (and, for the last-Mass-of -the-day crowd, perhaps for only a few hours), for this "Ash Wednesday." BUT THAT'S NOT ENOUGH! Ashes are not limited to a specially designated day of the week; ashes cannot be confined to some square on a liturgical calendar; ashes cannot be bounded by the size of one's forehead or one's thumb.

We may try to do our best imitation of Shakespeare's Lady Macbeth, who vigorously tries to wipe away the blood-stains of her murderous act, nearly rubbing her skin raw, shouting out at the top of her voice: "Out damn spot: out I say!"—but these ASHES, much like the spots on her soiled hands, are always here!

We are no strangers to ashes...

Even if we plant a mile of rose beds or erect new towers of glass and steel at the site of the World Trade Center, in defiance of everything and everyone who blesses terror and the taking of human life, divinizing those actions with twisted scripture misquotes...there will always be ashes.

Even if we pour money and humanitarian assistance into Afghanistan, or Columbia, or Haiti, or any number of places in our world...there will always be ashes.

Even if Food for the Poor miraculously leveled the "Riverton Dump" in Jamaica and turned it into a distribution center larger than the "Mall of America"...there will always be ashes.

Even if we settle our marriage in divorce or child custody courts...there will always be ashes.

Even when we sentence another human being to death or execute him or her, having our retribution and "justice"...there will always be ashes.

Even when we "put the past behind us"; even if we "have it out" with a co-worker and "clear the air"; even when we admit that "life goes on" after the passing of a loved one; even though we said and truly meant, "I'm sorry"... there will always be ashes.

Even when we "promise to change," and work at it with great rigor and commitment, turning the "promise" into a "fact"…there will always be ashes.

Ashes are hard to get rid of, are hard to clean up and wipe away. We try to deny them, refuse them, and minimize them because we believe they speak more of what one *was* and not what *is now*. But they are not simply remnants or shadows of things, or people, or experiences *past*—they are what IS NOW—we bear them—our world bears them...and the Cross of Christ tells us GOD BEARS THEM!

The crosses we wear upon our brows are never large enough, could never be large enough to mark all the "ashes" of our lives. Neither stroke nor gesture could be broad enough to trace out the breadth of the ashes we bear within and around us. Although it seems that once per year we have an almost insatiable desire to carry our stain in a most public way, nevertheless, we hope they'll be placed sparingly...and usually, they are. BUT THERE'S NO ESCAPING THEM.

We wear them as the Lenten journey begins anew… and, although not nearly as visible as on this sacred Wednesday, we wear they every day...to remember who we are; what we bring about; what we cause...and we wear them, most importantly, to remember who alone is capable of purifying and cleansing us. We bear the dark and dreary dust to remember who alone gathers up the ashes and into them breathes new life. Sitting in the ashes, if we stay there long enough, with enough patience and openness, we will meet the One who knows these stains more than we know them ourselves, the One whom the prophet Joel declares is "gracious and merciful, slow to anger, rich in kindness, and relenting in punishment (2:13)". In the ashes, we will meet the One who is no stranger to the dust and dirt of the earth, the One who reached into the primordial muck of the earth and fashioned its clay into a people, a people made in the "image and likeness" of the Creator.

But the purification and cleansing and washing and restoring do not happen, cannot happen until our ashes are faced and confronted; until our ashes are stirred up and named; until our ashes are grieved and wept over and mourned. In the words of the Psalmist, we must first know who we are and to whom we belong: "Have mercy on me, O God, in your goodness; in the greatness of your compassion, wipe out my offense, and my sin is before me always (Psalm 51)."

AND there are no exceptions, exemptions; no one is

spared from sitting in ashes. In fact, even the Son of God died amidst the ashes! Paul makes this clear in his Second Letter to the Corinthians: "For our sakes God made him who did not know sin to be sin, so that in him we might become the very holiness of God."

Jesus Christ, the only Son of God, covered himself in the ashes of a broken humanity as he hung upon the Cross of Calvary. And indeed, it seems that this very "tree of infamy" was planted firmly in the smoldering ash heap of Jerusalem's garbage dump, "outside the gates," as Hebrews tells us.

Ash Wednesday has passed. Yet, it is painfully clear, the ashes we wear do not stain us for a moment, or a day, or a "season". Rather, they mark us in every moment, in every day, in the course of every season.

Ashes are hard to get rid of, hard to clean up and wipe away.

Upon further reflection, perhaps all those who scurried to our campus ministry office (and all those who filled the churches this past Wednesday) each year, begging to be smudged with ash, had the right idea...even if they had it for the wrong reason!

To find our God, we must turn to the ashes...and sit in them for awhile...sit in them, most likely, longer than we desire or think is necessary. And here, in the gritty, choking, smoldering, distressing dust, *our* ashes—as well as those of our parish, our Church, our neighborhood, our workplace, our circles of friends and companions, our country, our world—must be faced...and named...and grieved...until we can humbly cry out: "Spare us, Lord; spare your people!" For it will be only then that "the Lord will be stirred to concern and take pity on his people!"

# ARE YOU "HUNGRY" FOR LENT?

I guess it usually proves to be true that we hear what we want to hear. The story is told of four-year old Gwen who, while sitting at the Sunday afternoon dinner table, was excitedly relating what she had learned earlier in the day at Sunday school. As she was ready to plunge into a big slice of her favorite cherry pie, she was instantly reminded of an important detail from the morning bible story she had failed to mention.

"I think Jesus was very lucky to meet the devil; I wish I could, too!" she exclaimed! Her family, although quite accustomed by now to Gwen's "unusual" insights, looked more than a little bewildered. When they asked her why she thought Jesus was so lucky and why she wanted to meet the devil, Gwen gave them a big, cherry-stained grin and replied: "Cause he got to spend 40 days having dessert!"

I wish I could be mistaken about the Gospel for the First Sunday of Lent the way Gwen was. I suppose I'd be more excited about the scripture if it were an invitation to

40 days of "dessert" rather than an invitation to 40 days in the DESERT!

"Jesus, ***full*** of the Holy Spirit, returned from the Jordan and was ***led by the Spirit*** into the desert for forty days." Since there were no witnesses to this event, we may conclude that Jesus himself told his disciples about this struggle that took place in the desert in order to teach them something. But why…why was he LED into this struggle, this confrontation with evil by the Spirit?

The answer seems simple if we look at what happened. Jesus was sent to the desert to FIND GOD and to FIND HIMSELF. Jesus had come to that point in his life where he had to make decisions and choices about who he was, who he would become, and he was intent on finding out who God was in his life.

Unlike Gwen's mixing of words, this was not time for "dessert," but rather a time to do without. Why is it so important that we learn that Jesus "ate nothing," that he was "hungry"? It would seems that if Jesus were being led to experience who God is and who he is called to be, then *he needed to make room for this experience.* He had to open up space within himself and to allow enough room for God to enter. He needed to be vulnerable, open and hungering for nourishment—otherwise, if he were already full, he would have had no need for something or someone else in his life.

Lent, almost always associated with some attempt at FASTING, truly is a time to embrace experiences of

HUNGER—our personal hungers, the hungers of our parish community, and the hungers of a world where too few people consume too much of the world's food, drink and material goods.

Lent is an invitation to willingly enter into a prolonged experience of hunger—not some superficial hunger created by skipping a meal on occasion, or doing without one's favorite candy bar or cookie, but rather the kind of hunger that we feel in our gut, that plays tricks on our minds, that squeezes and pricks our hearts. These are the effects that millions of our brothers and sisters who experience true hunger and thirst every day, as they long for adequate nourishment, have to confront and wrestle with.

A deep experience of hunger, however, is fraught with danger, temptation and fear, for our human drive is to seek nourishment, satisfaction, relief from our hunger. The confrontation that Jesus experienced will be ours as well when we touch our true hunger—because we will have to decide from where and *from whom will we seek our satisfaction.* Will we turn to God and the abundant food and drink that God provides...or will we turn to the overwhelmingly abundant sources of nourishment that, in the end, lead us only to our own self-satisfaction and away from God's hopes and desires? In a society such as ours, one that relies upon and incessantly fans the flames of *consumption*, there are many "answers" to our hungers which are far from nourishing, but rather bring about the destruction of our body and soul.

Would that Lent were a time for reveling in "desserts" rather than deserts. But in this our desert, if we choose to truly enter it with commitment and purpose, we will be fed and nourished by the *God Who Feeds!*

# TIME TO GO "UNDERGROUND"

Usually, I get a late start on Lent; at least that seems to have been the case as I look back on the past several years. I suppose, as a pastor, I spend more time prior to Ash Wednesday worrying about getting everyone else ready for Lent—lining up liturgies, reviewing Christian Initiation rituals, dividing up the ashes, pressing the purple clothes, deciding on adult prayer and enrichment, re-locating the rules on fast and abstinence—that before I know it, it's week number three of Lent, and I'm just getting focused on *my* spirituality!

Well, this year is different! In addition to focusing on the parish, I've given myself the leisure to think about *my Lent*, and where I might be going this year. And I've decided—after much thought, reading, and prayer—I'm digging in! This year, **I'm GOING UNDERGROUND!**

I intend to "go underground" in the sense of seeking more spiritual depth, delving further below my surface spirituality and routine activities, entering through the dark and hidden (and troubling) caverns of my spirit. While we still tend to imagine Lent to be the time for "giving up" or "adding on" for a few weeks—it is still the season that belongs most especially to the Catechumens—those preparing for Initiation into the Church. And so, those of us already baptized into Christ take our lead from them—and we pursue our self-and-community examinations because we too need recommitment to the waters of new life we have already received. To be baptized into Christ Jesus is to "go down with him"—so that we may one day rise with him to the fullness of God's life!

Although Jesus admonishes us through Matthew's Ash Wednesday Gospel to do our praying and fasting "in secret," rather than make a show of our Lenten efforts, at the moment, I'm not really taking my cue from these challenging words. Instead, I am moved by another image, a more recent spiritual experience.

This past summer, while on retreat in New Mexico, I had the good fortune of entering into two sacred spaces occupied centuries ago by Native Americans. These sacred spaces are known as "kivas," which is the Hopi word for "ceremonial room." While there is some scholarly debate about the full nature of these underground chambers, it is widely accepted that the kivas were the center of spiritual activity for the community (sorry, *men only*, though).

While on pilgrimage one day near the end of my retreat, I visited an amazing round, subterranean chamber once occupied by the Anasazi peoples, entering into it by descending a ladder poking out of a singular opening in the roof. With replicas of murals painted on the walls, a reconstruction of the Native American spiritual art that once graced the circular dirt walls, I felt as though I had entered a different world, a different plane of existence. In the center of the kiva, there was a hole in the floor, called a *sipapu* [SEE-pah-puh/Hopi], which symbolized the navel of the earth from which the ancient ancestors were said to have emerged when they entered the present world. Thus, the symbolic connection between the people and Mother Earth was given tangible form.

I keep a small replica of a kiva ladder in my office, and while meditating the other day about the path my Lenten journey might take this year, catching sight of the ladder, now draped with a century old Navajo birthing blanket, I was brought back in spirit to my August journey into the ancient kivas of the Pueblo and Anasazi peoples—and in doing so—I found my path—and thc challenge for this Lent.

Many ancient peoples have always looked deep into and beneath the earth for images of meaningful spirituality. Our own Christian faith shares this same exploration, as we celebrate the Son of God, Jesus the Christ, who had to "go underground" before being raised on high by the Father. In Jesus' words, "unless a grain of wheat falls to the ground and is buried, it remains just a grain of wheat." Or as St. Paul so starkly reminds us with his powerful question: "Do you not realize that you were baptized into Christ's death?" Yes, to recover our souls, we too must go underground, beneath the many veneers and protective surfaces with which we hide our true self—and meet our self and the God who dwells in the depths, face-to-face.

The great American mystical poet and spiritual seeker, Ralph Waldo Emerson, as Thomas Moore reminds us, said that "he couldn't have the 'elevation' [of spirit] that he wanted because he didn't have sufficient bottom (cf. *The Soul's Religion*)." In other words, Emerson knew that to "soar with the Spirit," we must first "get to the bottom," to go underground, to visit the depths of who we are.

But, as we know all too well, and why, even as I write these words, still safely distant from Ash Wednesday, I am already hesitant about my pending path—after all, journeys to the depths, our depths, are frightening. The dark, hidden, mysterious regions of our souls are fraught with memories and disappointments and losses we may shudder to encounter or revisit. There are "crypts" within each of us where we think we have laid to rest old wounds, lost loves, shattered dreams, sinful choices—and we want to stay clear of those cemeteries, lest what we thought was dead and gone isn't really so, and now may come back to trouble us once again.

I recall how tentatively I descended the rickety rungs of the kiva ladder on the sacred grounds near the Rio Grande River in Albuquerque, unaware of what I might find when I hit bottom, unprepared for the mysterious etchings on the walls I was about to encounter—the pictured-stories of past triumphs and defeats. And now, as the rungs of my ladder are about to be placed through the opening of this sacred Lenten season on Ash Wednesday, I know that once again my steps will be tentative, that the descent below the surface features of my life will be slow. But I pray that the strength of the Holy Spirit, who lives in the deepest part of who God has created me to be and to become, will allow me to enter this sacred space, to visit the depths, so that on Easter morning, I may truly know what it means to *rise with Christ.*

May your choices this Lenten season, too, find you willing to risk the journey "underground."

# THE SMELL OF PINE SOL

Every Friday morning I am greeted by a wonderful, refreshing scent as I enter my office. Early in the morning before I arrive, our parish maintenance custodians are busy tending to the parish offices, giving them a quick sprucing up after a full week of activity. I'm not sure they actually use the brand product Pine Sol, but it sure has the distinctive smell of the stuff. When I walk through that office doorway on Friday morning, I have two experiences. One keeps me anchored here in the present and one takes me back in time.

Starting every Friday morning knowing that some serious cleansing has gone on in my office provides a kind of creature comfort. The smell of the Pine Sol entering my nostrils tells me: it's fresh, it's clean, it's a new beginning. No matter what has gone on in there in the days preceding the great Friday morning cleanup, a pure and pristine aura fills the room—in a sense, a kind of purging seems to have occurred.

But I am also drawn backward in time by that not-to-be-ignored, all-too-recognizable scent. My grandmother Emma, amongst her varied and voluminous talents, wielded a mean scrub bucket and brush—and she had a penchant for Pine Sol! She scrubbed many a floor—not only in her own home, but in the homes of others as well. Even when she and my grandfather lived in an apartment building, my grandmother insisted on keeping the entry halls clean and fresh for the other residents. Once a week, she'd get on her hands and knees (the only *real* way to scrub a floor!) to scour the floors and stair risers with her beloved Pine Sol. Pushing open the building's doors upon our visits, I could always tell when she had been on one of her scrubbing missions, as the aroma filled the whole building, and provided that same sense of freshness, cleansing and yes, purging.

I think of the Lenten season and the Lenten journey as a type of Pine Sol experience! In anticipation of the cleansing and renewing waters of Easter baptism and the renewal of our commitment to follow Christ, we spend these days and weeks purging ourselves, with God's trusted hand of course, of all the darkness and sinfulness that keeps us from living the abundant life that Jesus came to deliver. One of our Elect (those preparing for the Easter sacraments) commented after celebrating the first "Scrutiny" ritual at 5pm Mass last Saturday, that he felt as though he had received a good "scrubbing" while he and the community prayed for the Elect to be delivered from evil and the destructiveness of sin. In these Lenten days, we pray for the grace of freshness, cleansing, and yes, purging.

We pray for a fresh beginning in recommitting ourselves to the promises of our baptism, to a more faithful giving of ourselves to the Lord and God's people. For many of us, our commitment to Christ needs constant rekindling, for we all lapse into laziness or doing the bare minimum (and sometimes *even less* than the minimum).

We pray for cleansing from the ravages of sin in our lives. Perhaps the image of sin as "dirt on our souls" has long gone out of favor, but there is a sense that when we are truly struggling with sin and temptation, we feel dirty, messy and as though we've been dragged through the mud. The Lenten season provides not only the Elect, but also all of us the opportunity for a good "scrubbing."

We pray for purging, as well, in order rid ourselves of the obstacles that prevent us from truly knowing and loving the Lord in our lives and in our relationships with others. Sometimes this purging comes by choice, and at other times, we are stripped and shown for whom we truly are in spite of our attempts to keep the façade working.

I look forward to Friday mornings—but not because it's the end of the week (after all, for a priest, Friday is merely the pause before the work-weekend)—but because for a few faint moments, I can breathe in a part of my past, as well as step into a new beginning. Indeed, this is our Pine Sol season, where God's gracious invitation to repentance and forgiveness wafts through the Lenten air we breathe, and where we are given the opportunity to soak it into our very beings—and once again to know ourselves and others as fresh, clean, and purged by the loving hands of God.

# MOVING "OUT" (NOT "IN") FOR LENT

Sometimes we think about our faith in Jesus Christ and our fellowship in the Body of Christ as if it were akin to belonging to a health club or gym! Our tremendous heritage of living the gift of faith down through the ages is a veritable treasure-trove of "Powerhouse" prayers, practices and persuasions.

Clearly portions of the Bible offer us athletic images with which to comprehend the gift of faith. Recall St. Paul speaking about "running the race," or about the kind of "nourishment" we take into our bodies. Throughout the history of Christian art, it is easy to trace the rise and fall of muscular portraits and sculptures of Christ, so much so that as one age became less comfortable with a Jesus on the "Ultra Slim Fast" plan, it was certain that a more robust, bicep-bulging Lord and Savior was not far behind! (I think of the recent uproar, at least in the *Letters to the Editor* of *The Florida Catholic*, over the all too "feminine" image of Jesus that was the winning entry in an art contest sponsored by the *National Catholic Reporter*). Spirituality movements in every era have often emphasized rigorous "workout regimens" for the body and soul, some severely disciplining the body and soul as a kind of retribution for sins.

If indeed Christianity has promoted a model of health club-like spirituality, certainly no season within the Church's rhythm of life seems more committed to getting the flabby faithful back on track than LENT! Lent is the season par excellence when we are asked to engage in a spiritual life check up, and upon finding our weaknesses and deficiencies, of which we always know there are plenty, we enter into a spiritual reconditioning program with an unusually high level of energy and concentration. Just look at the parish calendar of any Saint-so-and-so Church during the six weeks of Lent. Beginning with the pew bulging attendance at the numerous Ash Wednesday Masses and Prayer Services (what other "Wednesday" of the Church year would ever draw such a crowd?), the Lenten days are filled with a plethora of spiritual "growth" opportunities, more numerous than any other time of year. There always seems to be something for everyone: retreat days for men and women, special classes and discussion seminars, faith sharing groups, Stations of the Cross on Fridays, Eucharistic devotions, Penance services and extra confession times. Accompanying all these official workouts, there are the traditional personal practices of fasting, dieting, sacrificing, sharing alms for the poor in a special project, extra rosaries, novenas and devotionals, reading a spiritual book. Indeed, a rigorous tucking and toning awaits any member of the Christian community who has the courage and commitment to enter into the Lenten regimen.

Although upon close inspection, we might uncover that all this spiritual reconditioning and getting in shape benefits more than ourselves, our own personal spiritual physiques, it seems that the overwhelming focus of the Lenten disciplines and commitments centers upon an INTERIOR change or conversion. Our Lenten work-outs generally seem to involve a turning inward, a soul-searching personal quest for spiritual improvement. Even, at times, it seems that the Church as a whole takes an inward turn during Lent, as evidenced by the number of 'in-house," "at-the-church" activities that multiply during Lent; people simply spend more time IN church than at any other time or season of the year. Perhaps this individualized sense of spiritual growth, this turning inward takes its cue from the Ash Wednesday Gospel proclamation in which Jesus tells us:

*Be on guard against performing religious acts for people to see. Do not blow a horn…do not let your left hand know what your right hand is doing…keep your deeds of mercy secret…do not behave like the hypocrites…go to your room, close your door, and pray…groom your hair and wash your face. In that way no one can know you are fasting. . . (Matthew 6).*

All of this close, personal introspection is certainly a worthy undertaking. For people who are generally unreflective about the comings and goings of their lives, for people who rarely have time to think about decisions and choices, a disciplined time and environment which encourages turning inward can be a special blessing and welcome friend, despite the rigors this turning seems to require. Yet, there is another cue we often seem to miss from the clarion call that rings out from the Scriptures as Ash Wednesday breaks through the business-as-usual of our lives and summons us to new spiritual depths of experience. Lent is limited and crippled in its power to effect true change and conversion, the kind of Gospel metanoia that demands a radical about-face rather than a casual or wimpy "glance over my shoulder." The Lenten journey is depleted of its energy and strength to lead us to renewed awareness of the image and likeness of God that swells at the center of our very being when it remains merely an inward turning. The power of the Lenten wakeup call must be a significant TURNING OUTWARD!

While our normal Lenten practices and disciplines tend to challenge us to slowly pry open the gates of our souls and to enter more deeply down the spiraling staircase of our interior life, in reality, the end point of the Lenten journey leads us not in and through the interior gate, but rather OUTSIDE THE GATES, outside the camp, to the foot of the Cross! The death of Jesus, the bitter, stark fact that is the way to salvation, takes place not in a warm, cozy, romantic surrounding, portrayed as a candle-lit, death bed scene out of some Victorian novel, but rather it takes place amidst the squalor and degradation of a crucifixion mound outside the gates, far from any semblance of warmth, tenderness, or intimacy. Brutalized and naked, isolated and rejected, Christ hung on the Cross, suffering the death of a capital criminal.

Indeed it seems that the proper direction to follow, the more authentic course of rigor and discipline to pursue during Lent takes us OUTSIDE ourselves, beyond the warm confines of our own lives, the intimacy of our personal soul-centers, to those people and situations which are OUTSIDE THE GATES. Our Lenten journey ends as the Passion and Death of Jesus begins to unfold.

In order to grasp the full impact of this movement outside the gates, we may need to reappropriate the impact of the Cross and the whole crucifixion cxperience of Jesus.

As is the case with most symbols of religious faith, over time and through the routine that always settles into our experiences, we tend to domesticate, to tame the power of our icons of faith. While the Cross of Christ is clearly and undeniably central to our faith, there is a kind of coziness that springs up between believers and the symbol of the cross. While it is true that this "tree of death" is eventually transformed into a "tree of life," we must dwell a bit longer at the foot of the "tree of DEATH" if we are to reclaim its power to move us toward life! If we might recognize the guiding symbol of the now famous "star," westward leading, still proceeding, drawing and leading the Magi to Christ, as the premier icon of the Christmas season, it can be said that the premier icon of the Lenten season is the CROSS, guiding and leading us, beckoning us to follow it OUTSIDE THE GATES, outside our comfortable camps, and to meet the God who made the nearly incredulous decision to make God's dwelling outside the sanctuary of the temple, outside the safe confines of orderly and organized religious practices, traditions and disciplines. At the foot of the Cross, we rather meet the God who dwells most intimately with the outcast and abandoned, the isolated and disengaged, the rejected and the refused—who literally often become the *refuse*, the *garbage* of societies throughout the ages.

Yes, a more challenging path to follow this Lenten season may not involve a turning inward, but rather a turning outward, outside the gates of our holy cities, to the foot of the Cross, where God dwells with the alienated and suffering. Yet, to see this path, to enter more deeply into what this means for our spiritual well-being, we do need to reappropriate our understanding of the Cross and the crucifixion of Christ, to be reminded of its bitter degradation, to once again untame this striking folly of our faith and unleash its power to save, to allow this devastatingly foolish symbol of God's presence, which so many of us wear around our necks and upon our chests, to ignite a fire and burn a hole in our hearts, rather than simply rest gently upon our breasts.

In the Letter to the Hebrews, the invitation is proffered to us to go to Christ *outside the gates* and to meet him with all those who make their dwelling there:

> *The bodies of the animals whose blood is brought into the sanctuary by the high priest for the atonement of sin are burnt outside the camp, and so Jesus too suffered outside the gate to sanctify the people with his own blood. Let us go to him, then, outside the camp and share his degradation (Heb. 13:11-13, Jerusalem Bible trans.).*

The author of the Letter to the Hebrews is recalling the ancient celebration of reconciliation between God and God's people know as the *Day of Atonement*. It was the once-per-year ritual in which the high priest entered the inner sanctum of the holiness tent or the temple, wherein was housed the sacred Ark of the Covenant, the most physical embodiment of God's living presence among the people. With the blood of sacrificed animals, whose bodies were destroyed outside the camp, the priest and people where sprinkled as a sign of penance and restoration. Now, with the inauguration of the new covenant, it is no ordinary blood that is sprinkled, but rather the blood of the Son of God, Jesus the Christ, the new lamb, who is sacrificed so that the relationship between God and humanity might once again be restored to its fullness. Jesus is sacrificed upon the Cross outside the gates—and we are admonished to GO TO HIM OUTSIDE THE CAMP.

But what is this place of sacrifice where Jesus hangs? How might we reappropriate the meaning of the crucifixion? What will we find when we "go out to meet him" beyond the safety of the camp?

Robert Schreiter, C.Pp.S. plumbs this depth of meaning and unveils insight for us in his article "Outside the Gates" (in *The Wine Cellar*, February 1994), which reflects upon the above passage from Hebrews 13:

*Outside the camp was the garbage dump where the refuse of the community was pitched and burned. To that place was taken those things that were no longer of use to the community inside the camp…this place outside the camp stood for the very opposite of the organized and civilized life within the camp: inside was order, security, belonging, intimacy; outside were chaos, danger, alienation, and loss.*

*The image of the garbage dump would have had rather further poignancy for the first century readers because crucifixions were often held in garbage dumps. The Romans reserved crucifixion as a punishment for rabble rousers and those who threatened the public order that Rome imposed on its captive states. If was intended as an excruciatingly painful and ignominious way to die.*

*Crucifixion was not only a painful way to die; it was also deliberately intended to be a shameful death as well.*

*The stark statement in the Letter to the Hebrews points to a profound reversal of how we ordinarily understand the world to be.*

*To see the cross as the place that God has chosen to dwell represents a reversal of most of our values.*

*And as Hebrews reminds us, we cannot peer out toward the cross from the safe confines of camp. To experience the living God, we must go out of the gate, to meet Christ in the reproach that he suffers on the cross.*

If indeed Lent is for us a time of reorientation and metanoia, then our footsteps, albeit reluctantly, must trod the beaten path beyond the safe and secure confines of our well-ordered faith and casually repetitive Lenten practices of additional prayers and less sweets. To venture toward the Cross of Christ is truly a reversal of our usual direction.

In this light, perhaps our Lenten journey, our Lenten passage might concentrate on our *goings, our departures* rather than upon our entrances. A more authentic turning during this Lenten season is *outward*, beyond the routine of our revitalizing program of spiritual tucking and toning. The Cross stands as a constant, stark reminder about where God chooses to dwell…and to where we must go to meet God.

Although the dusty, dark ashen Cross, which is traced upon our brow as the great Lenten journey begins, quickly fades (or we wipe it off before going back into public), in reality, its mark is burned into our hearts. Perhaps we are foolish to wear so boldly this mark of infamy, yet it serves as the ultimate guide to where our steps will take us if we have the courage to make the journey—***outside the gates!***

# HOLY WEEK

*We are all most likely familiar with Michelangelo's powerful statue the Pieta, where we find Jesus resting in his mother's arms after he is removed from the cross. Despite his brutal death, Mary's face still conveys a deep and profound tenderness. Although the scene is frozen in chiseled marble, it is not hard to imagine, if one stares at the statue long enough, Mary caressing Jesus' lifeless and bloodied body with her weary arms. But what about Jesus resting in his Father's arms? Can we imagine such a scene? After all, one of the final phrases uttered by Jesus is, according to some Gospel narratives, "Father, into your hands I commend my spirit." In this Holy Week, we too are invited not only to utter these words, but to live into them: "Father, into your hands, we commend our spirits."*

# "A CLOSER WALK"

As the path of our Lenten journey begins to narrow, as the steps become more ominous in the days and weeks ahead, we are invited by the Lord to make a "closer walk." When Lent first broke on the scene, most likely we were filled with enthusiasm, commitment, and vigor. The starkness of the church decor and the striking purple draping looked refreshing and mysteriously soothing. The 40 days adventurously stretched out before us like the bricks on Dorothy's "Yellow Brick Road" in the Wizard of Oz. Fortified with our package of spiritual practices, our commitments to more regular prayer routines, our lighter than usual appetites for sodas and sweets, and the safety of distance from the ultimate end of Lent, Jerusalem "our destiny," we set out skipping to the tune of our own Lenten songs that would lead us "over the rainbow," arm in arm with members of our community who would travel a similar path.

But where are we now? Now that the path is becoming more harrowing, now that the road is looking more like the Way of the Cross rather than the way to the "Emerald City," now that the journey is marked with pain and suffering, are we still willing to make that "closer walk" with the Lord? Are we starting to scatter in the same way the disciples did? Are we any more committed to staying at his side than those who walked and talked with him on a daily basis? What is this "closer walk" to which we are invited? Is it too close for comfort?

With the approaching days of the Passion and Death of the Lord, the Scriptures take a decided turn toward the rigorous landscape through which Jesus had to pass on his way to Jerusalem. The sun and heat, the dirt and dust, the sleepless nights and emotionally exhausting days would tell only half the story of the stress Jesus experienced, for the other half that made the way dangerous and lonely was the gradual turning away of followers unwilling to make the "closer walk." As talk turned away from the glories of the Kingdom and God setting things in proper order, and now began to focus upon the unexpected truth that "the Son of Man must suffer and die," the once-followers began to seek their own paths, ones which diverted them from the road to Jerusalem. This kind of talk was too much for them; this kind of talk was too prophetic; this kind of talk scared them! The disciples wanted to skip the "three days" and leap right for the glorious climax, the "raising up by God." The "closer walk" which Jesus was now requiring of them was indeed too close for comfort; comfort would need to be found elsewhere—and elsewhere did they seek it.

At the San Pedro Retreat Center, there is a wooden "pier" that cuts a swath through the woods, ultimately ending on the craggy, secluded edge of a lake. The path is named "A Closer Walk." I have traversed this pathway many times since my arrival in Orlando; despite its gently winding twists and turns, it is a place where God has taken the opportunity to "set me straight," as I am sure he has done for many others who have ventured along these planks. A sign warns, upon entrance, "Slippery When Wet," but I have found that when one encounters God along the way, whether in the depth of meditation and prayer, or immersed in the words of Holy Scripture, or watching a spider spin its web amidst the tender branches of a neophyte palm, things can get pretty slippery even when it's been weeks without a drop of rain!

Because of the peace and serenity that sccm to rise up like vapor from the grounds of San Pedro, I simply took for granted that the name given to this particular pathway was a simple designation of one's journey with the Lord while spending a day or week in prayer at the retreat center. I even thought that perhaps, given the Franciscan's love for music, the forest path was named after the classic song, "A Closer Walk With Thee." Nestled in the beauty and wonder of God's creation at San Pedro, the invitation to make a "closer walk" seems easy and understandable—hardly threatening.

On a recent jaunt down "A Closer Walk," with the

days of the Lord's Passion weighing heavily on my mind and heart, suddenly I became more aware of the meaning of the name given to this pathway. As I gazed along the edges of the "pier," making my way slowly toward the lake, I saw something about the "beauty" of this stretch of God's earth that I previously hadn't allowed to wrest my attention. With each step, with each methodical shuffling of one foot after the other, **I took in, for the first time, the immensity of the BROKENNESS that littered this sylvan sanctuary.** For the first time, I was overwhelmed by the fact that the beauty of this pathway is not merely conveyed by the *life* springing up along the edges, the lush tropical foliage, the squirrels and birds that make their home there, but also by the *death* so intricately intermingled. The depth of the beauty was only fully recognizable when I was willing to absorb the brokenness and decay along with the vitality and vigor of the landscape. Now I began to understand more clearly why the path is known as "A Closer Walk."

***To walk more closely with God means to navigate along pathways strewn with life and death, weeds and wheat, rocks and sand, decay and debris—our own and that of others.*** So often, we look for only completeness and wholeness when we seek the Lord, but the Lord hears the cry of the poor and brokenhearted, and the Lord makes a home with the incomplete and unwhole, with the less than beautiful in the eyes of the world. To walk intimately with the Lord, to make a closer walk with God is to follow a path that reveals all the chips and cracks, all the corrosion and corruption that intermingles with the attractive and unblemished, with the smooth and pristine.

Henri Nouwen, a faithful seeker and disciple of the Lord who rarely shrank from taking an intimate look at every path God set before him, recognized all too well the inescapable presence of brokenness when walking with the Lord. He recounts in his *Sabbatical Journey*:

> *Our life is full of brokenness—broken relationships, broken promises, broken expectations. How can we live that brokenness without becoming bitter and resentful except by returning again and again to God's faithful presence in our lives* (134)?

The challenge of these closing weeks of Lent, of accepting the invitation to make a "Closer Walk" is to begin to see the beauty in our brokenness and know it to be loved and embraced by God.

# A PASSION SUNDAY TRYPTCH

## I

As a young college student, I was fortunate to have a wonderful Missionary of the Precious Blood priest as a mentor throughout my course of study at Saint Joseph's College. His name was Al Druhman. Of the many contributions Al made to my development as a person and seminarian, one of the most lasting has been my love for the theater. Not only was he an insightful professor of literature and drama in the classroom, but he often invited me and a few other students to attend plays with him. Thus, we were able to experience the thrill of seeing what were once only printed words on a page now brought to life on the stage.

The fact that drama, as we know it in the Western world, had its origin in the *religious* enactments of the ancient Greeks is not surprising. One does not have to develop too keen an eye to detect the close relationship between religion and drama even in our Christian faith tradition. Drama is at the heart of our faith.

As we walk the Palm-laden path this *Passion Sunday*, we are entering into the *drama* of Jesus' life. Our presence, however, calls for more than simply sitting in a tiered theater seat as a spectator, viewing the action from afar. No, we are called to **participate** in this drama, to step into the middle of it, and to become one of the actors! It is only by stepping INTO the story that we will be able to draw life from it.

In what way are you presently being called to enter into the drama of Christ's Passion and Death? How is this path reflected in your life? Can you see yourself in any of the scenes of the drama? Which character are you; with whom do you identify? Jesus speaks to many individuals and groups throughout the Passion accounts of the New Testament—what is Jesus saying to you?

## II

***Passion*** can be frightening for many people. Some may even consider passion a dirty word (I often wonder, are words really dirty, or is what we *do* with them that make US dirty?) Perhaps we too often associate living a passionate way with fanatics or extremists, people on the edge (about ready to fall off). So, in our desire not to be considered either dirty or fanatical people, we choose to live lives in mediocrity, at best, playing it safe down the middle of the road. If Jesus had chosen to live his life this way he never would have garnered any followers, never been questioned about his actions and beliefs, never been seen as a threat to anyone, and ultimately, he never would have been crucified! He basically would have passed his days in obscurity, soon to be forgotten with the passing of a few generations, just as happens to most of us.

Thankfully, Jesus chose to live his life with ***PASSION***, to engage the world at its most risky depths. I'm sure this is what attracted people to him—the fact that he lived his life to the full. After all, if, as John's Gospel tells us, Jesus came to "bring us life in abundance," then he must have been an example of abundant living in everything he said or did.

If only we could experience some of that ***PASSION*** ourselves. It is risky, though. People would certainly take notice of us, and perhaps even be drawn to us. That means extra responsibility (as if we don't have enough already). Yes, it is much safer to live in relative obscurity. It is more exhausting to expend the energy required of passionate living. But the richness of the gift(s) of life which God bestows on each of us is slowly eroded when we choose to live without passion.

When was the last time you can recall having experienced something with passion? When was the last time you gave yourself to someone or something with a fire burning within you? Perhaps the drama of Jesus' ***PASSION***, which we reenact this Holy Week, is our invitation to die to all within us that settles for mediocrity and to embrace the abundance of living offered by God.

## III

The Passion account found in the Gospel of Mark, like all of Mark's narrative, is simple, direct, and at times, stark. Not a lot of fluff, not a lot of filler, not a lot of lofty theologizing (like we find in John's account, read on Good Friday)—Mark, one could say, seems to echo the famous words of Detective Joe Friday in the old *Dragnet* series: *The facts, ma'am, just the facts!* In reading and reflecting on Mark's Passion narrative, I came across a commentary by one scripture scholar which struck a chord with me. In the author's study of Mark, chapter 15, he points out that at the moment of Jesus' death, he cries out in Aramaic, which was his native language. It was also the language spoken by his closest friends and followers. Yet, as Mark illustrates, *no one who hears his voice can understand what he says!* Jesus dies on the cross utterly abandoned, executed among "strangers."

What a powerful scene Mark paints. Jesus experiences the kind of death which all of us fear—dying utterly alone! The circumstances of his death, however, are reflective of the pattern that had begun in the weeks and months leading up to this climax of the drama—people were gradually having a harder time understanding him. He was speaking the words, offering the gestures of healing and compassion, embracing the weaknesses of all who came to him—yet those who came did not grasp the real purpose of it all! They wanted to maintain the superficiality of their relationship with him; all this talk of dying and rising, being lifted up, laying down one's life for friends was too much!

As we cross the threshold of this Holy Week, are we unable to hear and understand the words Jesus is speaking to us? Is it a language we recognize, yet a language we prefer to ignore? Are we gathering as a community of followers who know and embrace his words, or are we a company of strangers, looking on from a distant hill, maintaining what we believe to be just enough contact to insure a shot at salvation? As we reenact the drama of Jesus' passion and death, his final days, will we also be reenacting the abandonment of him who comes to give us life? And when Easter morning dawns, will we find ourselves, dressed in our Easter finery, in the hypocritical position of now running to embrace the risen Christ (now that all the pain and suffering have passed), the same Christ whom, only a few days earlier, we did not recognize?

# THE STATIONS OF THE CROSS... STEPS TOWARD RESPONSIBILITY

On the evening of the first Friday of Lent, I engaged in something I have not done for years—making the Stations of the Cross. All sorts of memories came alive as I traversed the path around our church, staring at the wood carvings on the wall, singing a verse of song, kneeling in prayer.... I recalled assisting the priest as a Server, carrying the cross in procession from station to station; although we sang a different tune that night, the melody of the *Stabat Mater* rang in my ears; I reminisced about quietly praying the stations at home, or accompanying my grandparents to church for this devotional practice; I'm sure, somewhere along the way, I have colored numerous pictures of scenes from the stations; I've experienced the stations through many media: acted out in words by costumed players, made life-like in bloody detail by the Spanish-speaking community of Chicago on several Good Fridays as we traversed the "Social Justice" versions of the Stations—stopping at various public buildings to recall the injustices perpetrated in the lives of people by multinational corporations, penal institutions and governmental agencies. I'm sure you have your own memories.

I suppose the most striking feature of this most recent experience of the Stations of the Cross was the overwhelming sense of responsibility that Jesus claimed as he made his way from Pilate's judgment hall to Golgotha, the Place of the Skulls. He claimed his cross—although it was a cross he did not cherish, did not exactly choose himself; a cross that was thrust upon him, yet a cross he embraced of his own free will. The Lenten experience, particularly reflected in the lives of those preparing to make a faith-filled commitment to the Catholic community at the Easter Vigil, yet an experience to which we are all called to avail ourselves, is an invitation to claim responsibility, to take the steps necessary to lay claim to our lives, our experiences, our strengths and weaknesses, and to face ourselves for who we are...and then...to DO something about what we discover!

As I reflect upon the "steps" Jesus took, so poignantly captured in the "Stations" of the Cross (the WAY of the Cross), I am reminded of another set of steps that people take in order to claim responsibility for their lives—the "Twelve Steps." Yes, the Twelve Steps of Alcoholics Anonymous, now so appropriately and fruitfully applied to many other "recovery" programs, is a wonderful model for all of us in the challenges we face in claiming responsibility in our lives. From the opening step of "admitting our powerlessness," to "making a searching and fearless moral inventory of ourselves," to the "twelfth" step of "carrying this message to others and to practice these principles in all our affairs," people engage in a journey toward greater responsibility.

As Richard Rohr wrote in ***Breathing Under Water; Spirituality and the 12 Steps***, "we are all afraid of the radical self-responsibility of the Twelve Steps. No blame, no denial, no toxic shame, just the honest statement, 'I am a ________________.'" Perhaps the thrust of our Lenten journeys may be an exercise in "sentence completion," like the one Rohr proposes. Perhaps we will have the courage through our acts of prayer, fasting and almsgiving to uncover "who" we really are, and to claim responsibility for ourselves, our actions, our words, our thoughts—both what we do and fail to do.

Perhaps the greatest insight, the most powerful step we may be able to take toward growth and renewal this Lent will be the step which allows us to claim, for example, "I am an abuser; I am controlling of others; I am constantly jealous; I am vindictive; I am a person who always blames others; I am unfaithful; I am lazy; I am racist; I am a complainer." Each of us can make our own "I" statement, and then move on to the other steps that begin the process of DOING something about what I have claimed for myself.

The "Twelve Steps" are powerful...ask anyone who is successfully navigating recovery. Perhaps we should have these "steps" or "stations" etched along the walls of the church. Jesus' path to Calvary was his "fourteen"-step route to responsibility. For in claiming his cross, in bearing it without blame, denial or shame, he was embraced by God and raised to new life.

What must you and I lay claim to in our lives, at this moment; what is it that each of us is being challenged to claim responsibility for, so that we too may experience the new life of God on Easter morning?

# WHERE HAVE ALL THE PALMS GONE?

I am not very astute with song titles and artists. I can easily recognize a song when I hear it, but that's about as far as it goes. Usually what I do, when the subject of title and artist come up, I simply dip into my *very* short list of songwriters/singers and throw out one of their names. Rarely am I ever correct...but at least my contribution often gets a laugh!

As we begin the path to Jerusalem in this holiest week of the year, I cannot help but imagine Jesus' disciples singing their own version of the 1960s hit: *Where Have All the Flowers Gone?* (Sorry...can't remember the artist! Was it Johnny Cash? Petula Clarke? Cher?) Had the lyrics been available, I can picture the disciples, huddled in some corner of the city of Jerusalem, lamenting amongst themselves, most likely out of Jesus' earshot: *"Where have all the PALMS gone?"* Sure didn't take long for the passionate waving of palm branches to degrade into the angry, bitter waving of fists. Sure didn't take long for the glad *Hosannas* to be replaced with stinging cries of *Crucify him! Crucify him!* Indeed, the ride of triumph quickly turned into the walk of tragedy. Jesus' ride upon a blanket-draped donkey, listening to the cheers of the crowd was all too speedily replaced with the blood-stained trek toward the isolation of the cross, listening to the jeers of his enemies.

None of us have experienced quite the dramatic shift in acceptance that Jesus did on his way to Jerusalem, but it is not hard to identify with our own encounters in life when we too have felt like singing, "Where have all the palms gone?" Each of us has most likely faced events in our lives when "everything" seems to have changed. Each of us has had to struggle with that speedy or even gradual movement from joy to sorrow, from high expectation to bitter disappointment, from the novelty of new beginnings to the nadir of being stuck in the seemingly endless middle of things.

Some of the occasions come all too easily. Who amongst us cannot look back at specific events in our lives when we too were riding high in the saddle of joy and satisfaction, even to the point of garnering accolades from those around us for a job well done? Remember the glorious feelings of the day your first child was delivered, or you walked down the aisle toward a life-long commitment to married love, or you started fresh at a new job, or settled into your exciting responsibilities as chairperson of a much-loved service organization, or greeted your students on day one of a yet-unscathed school year? The list can go on.

## WHERE HAVE ALL THE PALMS GONE?

Surely we remember the "palms" we waved or were being waved upon our arrivals into these new beginnings, brimming with unlimited expectations, hopes, dreams and energetic commitments. Perhaps even a *Hosanna* or two fell from our lips as we nestled into our fresh starts and saw endless possibilities stretching out before us. Yes indeed, *palms* are part of our lives, and we are grateful for them.

However, not unlike Jesus' experience of reversal, we too have known the sadness of palms exchanged for pain. Who has not seen the giddiness of those first baby showers exchanged for adolescent rebellions? Who has not wept unceasing tears for broken relationships that no longer possess the love of a wedding day? Who hasn't seen colleagues move from expressions of joyful welcome for our presence to hard-edged complaints seeking our removal? Who hasn't witnessed the dashing of dreams, the cracking of commitments, or the fading of hopes? Who hasn't known the agony of any number of paths we've traveled in our lives where the palm-waving has been all too short in duration compared to the struggle with rejection and disappointment? Who amongst us couldn't sing from memory our own words to the tune, *Where Have All the Palms Gone?*

In a sense then, we should not be strangers to the drama that begins our celebration of Holy Week. Most of us have seen our once palm-laden paths deteriorate into treacherous trails. Most of us have heard the changeover from *Hosanna* to *Who do you think you are?*

But is there anything in Jesus' entry that can assist us when we face hopes and dreams that come crashing down?

Clearly there is much light that Jesus' entry into Jerusalem can shed upon our own confrontations with darkness, but two qualities seem most evident: Jesus draws upon a **commitment** deep within his spirit, and this commitment is based on a **relationship** with the One who never abandons us in the midst of turmoil.

Jesus did not judge by appearance, and he constantly cautioned his disciples to be wary of such judgments. He constantly spoke about putting on the "eyes" of God, so as to correct the myopia that comes from relying purely upon our human way of seeing. The disciples immediately got caught up in the wild and frenzied *Hosannas* and their complete misreading of the final end that Jesus was to meet. But Jesus' **commitment** was hardly based upon the events that occurred on the surface of his life; his commitment grew from deep within his soul. Jesus' commitment to the vision of God's Kingdom was embedded in him in such a way that neither palms nor pain could sway him from his path. While buffeted by the winds of acceptance and rejection throughout his ministry, Jesus never relinquished his grip on that inner commitment to the vision of his heart. Yet, he was only able to "see what God sees" because of his **intimate relationship** with God, a relationship forged through constant communication with God.

Like it was for Jesus, as we continue on our "procession," the journey of our life path, there will be palms… but there will also be passion. But in the end, it will take **passion** to persevere, a passion built upon a deep commitment in our hearts, nurtured by a faithful relationship with God.

# EASTER

*A friend once said, while being stirred in the depths of her soul at the baptism of adults during the Easter Vigil, "I wish I could jump back in that font and have that happen to me again!" The truth is—we can! The waters of the sacred font at Easter are not only meant for the newly initiated; they are meant for us all, for our parched and weary souls must once again be made soft and supple, so that we might go forth and make disciples, witnessing to the power of the Resurrection in our lives. Alleluia!*

# ONE DARK, WILD AND WET NIGHT—THE EASTER VIGIL

Sometimes it happens in an intimate moment: we stand, facing the truth…and we lack words…have no gestures which are adequate…no signs nor symbols to ease our struggle. AND YET, we feel no words, no gestures, no signs nor symbols would come close to conveying the whole meaning, for to consume the length and breadth of the meaning would be to swallow the sky above us. We face the terrifying truth that we must enter alone and face this moment of revelation, unencumbered and unprotected.

In the all-enveloping darkness of Easter's Vigil, we come face to face with the truth—lacking adequate words, gestures, and signs. And yet, we try to squeeze what we can from our feeble languages of words…kindling the brightest fire…unraveling the patchwork-quilt which tells the stories of salvation, bound by the single thread of God... splashing in the purest, most refreshing water...shouting the loudest "Alleluia!" And yet—even these cannot convey the whole meaning, the wondrous truth with which we stand face to face as Easter breaks upon the horizon.

We return to the place where a man died…and instead of death, we find LIFE! We return not to his demise, his end, as many suspected, but to his beginning, the place where he is born again—a birth into a new way of living that has no end.

It is no wonder, in the face of such truth, that we enter dazed, frightened and confused, as did the women, who were expecting no more than facing the daunting dilemma of rolling back the stone which sealed in the stench of death and decay. We return to the place where a man was bound and buried, wrapped in a death cocoon until his bones would turn to dust—and we are faced with an empty tomb…and the shattering, dizzying, utterly maddening words: "HE IS NOT HERE; HE HAS BEEN RAISED UP!"

In an eerie, mysterious, and sharply penetrating way, the words of those bedazzled messengers of God, which like an earthquake, rumble down through the centuries, stirring the brittle bones of all the dead, and reverberate against the walls of the souls of feeble believers gathered on a Jubilee Vigil night, in this most sacred of spaces. The thunderous proclamation splits open our hearts, and leaves us teetering on the edge of an open chasm…an open and now empty tomb: "Why do you search for the 'Living One' among the dead? HE IS NOT HERE; HE HAS BEEN RAISED UP!"

This is the truth that turns us upside down: that we

should find life in a place of death; that triumph is rising like a Phoenix from the smoldering ashes of failure and defeat.

This wild tale, this incredible testimony, this TRUTH... if we are honest before God and one another...SEEMS LIKE NONSENSE; it seems like NONSENSE and so often, we refuse to believe it!

How many times have you and I raced forward or backward to seek the living among the dead? How many times have we allowed a tomb to hold us bound? Why do we search for the living among the dead?

We do so because we FORGET—we forget the truth: "HE IS NOT HERE; HE HAS BEEN RAISED UP!"

How many times have you and I spent our last ounce of energy in pursuit of the living among the dead? There are those times when we have spent our last breath and shriveling spirits rehashing failed, dead relationships, blaming ourselves or others, thinking that sheer desire will fill them with life once again.

How often have we sought love from a particular person, who in her or his own weakness has been unable to return it—and we have sorrowed, and become bitter, and yet we've continued to look for love from them until our hearts have completely broken and despaired.

Often our pursuits of stocks and bonds, cars and homes, clothes and vacations, promotions and raises have failed to give us the fullness of life we long for—yet we keep looking for life amidst that which cannot give it.

Perhaps we have tried to return to the faith of our childhood, to those soft, sweet memories of Jesus as we "lay ourselves down to sleep," and have found them to be inadequate, unable to give us the life we need so desperately as adults. We wonder why we can find no life in a way of believing that is now no more than a distant memory, sandwiched somewhere in a scrapbook between our old communion veil or tie and our Senior Prom ticket stubs.

We search for words of truth, words to console and refresh us, words to build us up and make us strong, words to invigorate us, but we seek those words from every place but THE WORD, the Word of God, made flesh, living and breathing in the Scriptures, the sacraments, and communities called church, where sinful, yet faith-filled people make their way toward God and one another in mutual forgiveness and grace.

Look into your own life…see the ways in which you have been seeking the living among the dead…and tell me what NONSENSE is!

In the eyes of many, what we do in the darkness of the Vigil night is sheer, utter nonsense. Perhaps in some corner of our own hearts, the pin of nonsense is still pricking us.

As the gentle flicker of candles slowly drives the darkness away, as the *Lumen Christi* is thrice plunging into the flowing waters of the font, as wide-eyed visionaries, known to the Church as the Elect step forward and commit themselves and, in the eyes of the world, and yes, even in the eyes of some who see the Church of Christ as a dying institution, make the most nonsensical act of their lives—they pass through the humble birthing waters of the womb of the Church…and they emerge a NEW CREATION IN CHRIST! Most likely, as they have retraced their faith journey over these weeks and months of preparation, they have faced the absurdity that God would have finally led them to the Vigil night and the Easter sacraments. I am certain there were those who told them their journeys were nonsense…foolish dreams…a last ditch effort to make life a little more bearable.

The whole Church joins with the newly baptized... and with God's people throughout the world on this holy Easter morning…and from this moment on—our ignorance closes behind us like the doors through which we enter the church. Never again will we return to the place where a man or woman dies and find what we expect. Instead of death, we find life! We find not our end, but our beginning, the place where we are born again.

Love endures beyond all coming and going, beyond even the doors of death!

Sometimes it happens: we stand facing the truth and lack the words…have no gestures…no sign; and yet—we feel—no word, no gesture nor sign can adequately convey the awesome TRUTH we possess.

We peer into the empty tomb…and we face this, our moment of revelation: STOP looking for the living among the dead…allow the grace of God to raise you up and see the light of Christ penetrating whatever darkness you find yourself wrapped in.

DON'T JUST STAND THERE…PEERING INTO THAT BLACK HOLE IN AMAZEMENT…GET ON YOUR WAY…TELL IT TO EVERYONE: JESUS CHRIST IS RISEN TODAY, ALLELUIA!!

# FROM THE DARKNESS OF DEATH SHINES NEW LIFE:
## *THE REBIRTH OF A CHERISHED RELATIONSHIP*

With the taste of death deep in my throat, and the vicarious pangs of loss wrenching my stomach, I once again became acquainted with a truth that most of us work strenuously to avoid—that in close proximity to death, we uncover the power of life! A phone call from a friend in Cincinnati left behind words of sorrow on my answering machine a couple of weeks ago: "Ben it's John...Jimmy's dad, Mr. Seidler, died of cancer! It was fast. . .only a month! Just wanted to let you know. Call me...."

I was stunned! "Mr. Seidler" was the father of a dear friend, Jimmy, whom I forged a friendship with many years ago, in the earliest days of my college ministry. It was the kind of relationship that so serenely unfolds between two kindred spirits, the kind of bond that can only be forged between people sharing a college residence hall, somehow trying to maintain one another's dignity and strength amidst the raucous and sometimes rank setting of dorm life. As I entered beyond the doorpost of Jimmy's personal life and came in touch with his family, especially his mom and dad, I knew I had found yet another "home away from home," the kind of safe place that the Lord always seems to be providing those of us who have chosen to serve God and the Church in the celibate Roman Catholic priesthood, those of us about whom Jesus said, "there is no place to lay one's head"—at least not permanently and devotedly.

My first pang, interestingly enough, was not for Mr. Seidler (also named "Jim") but for my friend Jimmy. In many ways, I was happy for Jimmy's dad—since I knew that his long nightmare had ended and his deepest dream was now commencing—the end of the deep, abiding pain and somewhat aimless wandering after the loss of his precious wife Diane, who died several years earlier (at the age of 53)—and the beginning of the kingdom party about to be celebrated upon their reunion in God's bountiful reign. It seemed like only yesterday that I held and cried with the members of Diane's family as tortuous decisions were made about life-support options for her...only a wisp of memory separating the today of life and the day I presided over Diane's funeral liturgy and buried Jimmy's mom in Chicago.

In all honesty, I mourned for Jimmy...and I longed to talk with him...especially since we had not been in touch with one another for several years! When I first moved to

Florida, there were the usual, periodic phone calls...then only the Christmas cards...and then...nothing. I couldn't even get back in touch with Jimmy because I had lost, and had no way of locating, a phone number or address (he had already moved several times)—even a search through the Internet failed to produce what I needed. Through the lost time and the strained tendons of friendship, I had begun to resign myself to another "death"—the death of this friendship, one that had held so much meaning and beauty at a previous twist in the path of my life.

Yet, the intimate proximity between death and life shone once again, as the relationship that had been "buried" between Jimmy and me, was called out from its tomb, no less dramatically, and with no less emotion, that the thunderous shout of Jesus, calling to his dead friend: "Lazarus...Come out!" After getting back in touch with my Cincinnati connection, another friendship dating back to his college days and my back-to-school ministry as a priest, I reconnected with Jimmy—and LIFE was breathed back into the "dry bones of Ezekiel's vision," which our cherished relationship had come to reflect.

New life...so intimately proximate to death.

Perhaps, one may scoff at the experience and meaning of such reunions. After all, don't we cajole and tease one another at weddings and funerals with the now infamous question-phrase: "Why is it we only meet under these conditions? How sad!" I do not propose to know the answer, although I have had, over many years, to personally struggle with this question, a question that rises up like a thief in the night every time I have had to find my way from one community of ministry to another, from one city or town to another. Yet, I have found that the "answer" to the "why?" is not as important as what one does when faced with opportunities to rediscover life amidst the ruins of death. The query "why?" of the dry bones pales in comparison to the more perplexing, yet potentially exhilarating queries, "now what?" or the "can life be breathed into these dry bones?"

I'm not certain why we seem so shocked when confronted with the intimate proximity between death and life—it is a quite regular occurrence, not so unusual an encounter. Perhaps our defenses are so high and always on alert against any talk or mention of death, whether our own or someone else's, that we pretend that death is only about death, not life, and so we resist to acknowledge this intimacy. As the spiritual giant Henri Nouwen challenged us to see, death is not an *intruder*, catching us by surprise... but is rather the *doorway* to new life, the natural consequence of our living in this created world. For Nouwen, death bonds us in a "great human sameness" *(Our Greatest Gift: A Meditation on Dying and Caring).*

Through the death of Jimmy's dad, when I came in touch, once again, with this truth, and I experienced it as real and tangible, not merely some philosophy or misplaced religious fantasy, I suddenly became more aware of other, both previous and recent, encounters with this truth. As members of our parish community gathered in a prayer vigil around the bed of a dying parishioner, also ravaged by cancer in a moment's notice, I saw and heard the chords of LIFE, not death, as the dominant song being sung. As I sat with a man in his home and heard him wax eloquently about the peace and serenity he has in the depth of his soul as he teeters between life and death, I was touched by a person who is already embracing, in Cardinal Bernardin's words, "death as my friend." As a lost teenager feels the heart- piercing sword of his first (of many) failed love, and struggles with the naked vulnerability and foolishness this has exposed in his life, seeds of how to love and live are already being planted for the next beautiful, caring relationship to which he will give himself. Despite his pain, there is already talk of "the next time." Life...in such close proximity to death. As I gaze upon the landscape of my home, mourning the devastation wrought by our drought and the freezes of this past winter, upon closer inspection, and even after the necessity of pruning, the introduction of a further act of "death-dealing," I now see green buds or a lonesome leaf, as tender and frail as anything new struggling to be born, blossoming forth.

As we race toward Easter in this coming week, this "Week" Mother Church owns as the "holiest of the holy," let us not leap over the truth that is unveiled before the tomb is rent open and our Savior emerges victorious—let us not pass over the truth that life and death are in intimate proximity to each other. Before Easter...we must savor death, for if we avoid the "death," we may lose our way to LIFE in the FULL.

This truth does not dismiss the reality of our struggle with it, for with death, there is still a great "unknown." In Henri Nouwen's words:

*We hesitatingly come forth out of the darkness of birth and slowly vanish into the darkness of death. We move from dust to dust, from unknown to unknown, from mystery to mystery. We try to keep a vital balance on the thin rope that is stretched between two definitive endings we have never seen or understood (Creative Ministry).*

Jesus' words to Peter will one day be our words. We too will experience that one day we "will stretch out our hands, and another will gird us and carry us where we do not wish to go." Death will inevitably "bind us" and lead us where, upon first blush, we do not wish to go. Yet, where it leads us is our ultimate home and happiness.

As we are invited this "Good" Friday to face the stark, desolate figure of the Cross, we confront the great mystery of our faith, of our life experience—in close, intimate proximity to death...is LIFE. Even the Resurrection doesn't *answer* the mystery, for mystery is meant not to be answered, but rather to be entered into as one would a labyrinth. Again, Nouwen's words are illustrative:

## FROM THE DARKNESS OF DEATH SHINES NEW LIFE

*The resurrection doesn't answer any of our curious questions about life after death, such as how will it be? How will it look? But it does reveal to us that, indeed, love is stronger than death. After that revelation, we must remain silent, leave the whys, wheres, hows, and whens behind, and simply trust (Our Greatest Gift).*

And so...although deeply moved and filled with joy and excitement, I remain silent in the face of the new life breathed into a once-dormant relationship with my friend Jimmy—silent not out of fear or dread or disbelief or mistrust or cautious optimism—but silent in the awesome face of the power of love to endure.

Be not so consumed with words (and there will be plenty of them as we gather and celebrate the Triduum liturgies) in these holiest of days ahead, but rather wrap your heart and soul around the silence, so that the silence may envelope you with its power and insight. Get close to the power of death...feel the agony and destruction wrought by the Cross....enter the Mystery with silent reverence. ..or else miss the opportunity for NEW LIFE!

"Mr. Seidler" left a tremendous legacy of life and love, one that will not soon be forgotten by those of us who knew and loved him, who cherished his warmth and friendship, who were inspired by his compassion and dedication to being a man for others. But his death has also become a gift—the gift of new life!

# AN EASTER MEMORY:
## *MY SISTER BETH'S "SAMPLE BASKET"*

In retrospect, I can look upon this childhood Easter memory of the "sample basket" with much amusement, although if I'm honest with myself, at the time of my youth, the case of the "sample basket" most likely led to shedding many a tear on Easter Sunday, as well as suffering through some unwanted, though richly deserved punishment.

My brother and I, being the greedy older siblings that we were, loved to preserve the quantity of goodies in our own Easter baskets by eating from our sister's Easter basket! Now, we were not so bold as to indulge whenever we felt like it—no, we were much more methodical, much sneakier! We raided it when she least expected. However, we made a series of fatal mistakes. You see, sometimes we didn't like the particular piece of candy we selected. After taking a bite, we quickly realized that we had no further interest in it. Rather than quietly disposing of it in the trash, for some unknown reason, we simply returned it, unwrapped, still wet from our taste-testing, into my sister's basket! As you might imagine, when my sister returned to her basket and found several pieces of slightly eaten candy covered with Easter straw, she made no small scene. When confronted by my parents about our foolishness, my brother and I responded with the only logic we could muster: "Well...her basket is the sample basket!" How were we supposed to know whether or not we liked a particular piece of candy if we didn't sample it first—and her basket was the one we designated for sampling!

Needless to say, this "logic" was severely inadequate, and the appropriate consequences were doled out! I learned a big lesson from this part of my history—be smart enough to throw away the evidence if I sneak into someone else's Easter basket and find something I don't like!

In recalling the "sample basket," I stopped to consider how often we look upon the Church as a giant sample basket. There it is, all pretty and filled with every kind of "candy" that we might need to make it through life, to make us feel good and sweet about ourselves and our lives. And we proceed to pick and choose our way through its bounty, although when we encounter something we do not like, something that leaves a bad taste in our mouths, we quickly toss it back. Sometimes our solution to this problem is to make up our own *basket* and to fill it only with the things we like or enjoy, leaving out all the things that make us uncomfortable or do not appeal to us.

The Church is no Easter basket, but rather it is a community of vast diversity and taste, made up of the sweet and not-so-sweet, the palatable and the non-palatable. While our tendency is to choose only that which we like, we are constantly reminded that the Church is much larger than personal tastes and preferences.

# FAR BEYOND "COFFEE ON THE TABLE AND BUTTERING BREAD":

*MUSINGS ON RESURRECTION*

*"Christ has risen." Whoever believes that*
*Should not behave as we do,*
*Who have lost the up, the down,*
*the right, the left, heavens,*
*abysses,*
*And try somehow to muddle on, in cars, in beds,*
*Men clutching at women,*
*women clutching at men,*
*Falling, rising, putting coffee on the table,*
*Buttering bread, for here's another day.*
*Czeslaw Milosz*
*(From "Six Lectures in Verse, Lecture V")*

In my own mind and heart, lurking somewhere behind the bombast and euphoria of the joy of the Easter tomb-explosion, there is, as Czeslaw Milosz has written, a lot of "coffee on the table and buttering bread." Despite the magnitude of Resurrection, I generally watch it creep into the recesses of everyday living—a move that almost certainly guarantees its obscurity and loss of power in confronting each day's deaths. As I ponder and celebrate *this* Resurrection season, I am beginning to have a clue about it all, and I sense the deeper challenge.

It's not that I doubt or despair of Resurrection (although there are surely grounds on which to have heavy doses of both)…it's that I want it NOW! No, not for me, but for the *Lazaruses*, the deep and devoted soul-friends and life-sustainers, who have been sealed behind their own stone-cold tombs for too long already.

I particularly long for my own garden-encounter with my grandmother Emma, where in the midst of my double-digit years of sorrow, I might hear her softly call out my name, see her gaze upon me with the warmest eyes I've known, and then have her enlarged heart (the condition that led to her death) pulsate its overwhelming love into every bone and ounce of flesh that I am. I wouldn't even mind the warning "do not to *cling* to me." I could deal with that, if in exchange, it meant a palpable face-to-face in the here and now.

I'd come running, even at the slightest scent of a pan-sauté of fish along some sandy shore, if it meant a reunion with my dearest friend, Fr. Stan Cmich, whose life ended from cancer after only two years a priest, coming just 6 weeks before he was to preach my first Mass. A Resurrection breakfast of any kind, served up with his long-mourned certainty of acceptance, would make *new life in Christ* all the more present on *this* side of the Kingdom.

While my soul stirs for another encounter, a trumpet (or even a whisper) from beyond the tomb, I deeply pray this Easter season that I don't allow Resurrection to melt into yet one more "so-what-else-is-new" numbness, the kind of which already over-populate my life. I want to, in the words of Wendell Berry, to ***practice resurrection*** in the here and now...to allow new life and the power of vivid memory to crack the seals that imprison the *Lazaruses* of my life, those whose loss continues to trouble and disturb me, and for whom, no matter the miniscule or mammoth years that may have passed, I still weep and mourn.

My loved ones do indeed rise from their tombs whenever I embrace the Jesus who rises in me—not merely in some future just beyond the edge of my straining eyes, but in the present moment of *falling and rising* on this side of the Kingdom to come.

Indeed, those of us who, in this tomb-quaking season, proclaim full-throated, "Christ is risen," should not behave as we so often do. For truth be told, today is *not* just another day of *coffee on the table and buttering bread.*

# LIVING THINGS HAVE THEIR WAY OF BREAKING THROUGH

The transition from vacation-mode back to real-life-mode isn't easy, despite every effort we make to keep the memories alive. There are, however, some folks (I've known a few) who get tired of the freedom they enjoy during an escape from their routines and who count down the days to their return with the enthusiasm of a child waiting Christmas Eve. As to those who have never learned the fine art of vacationing, all I can say is...poor souls!

This is not my problem at all. In fact, as the years go by, I find it increasingly more difficult to get back into the swing of things. I look at returning from time off much the same way I do "power napping" (which I've never been able to master). In my ill-fated attempts to power nap, always with its promise of awakening refreshed and ready to take on the world, all I have concluded is this: the longer I nap, the more I want to keep it going. Fifteen minutes of sleeping bliss never leaves me re-invented; it simply just makes me want another fifteen...and then fifteen more…and so on. My vacation experiences produce the same effect. The more I enjoy my time away, the more of it I long for. Who knows what would happen if I ever traveled for a whole month—I might never return at all! Cruising through my vacation fantasy land, I often imagine how easy it would be to never work again—and then of course, that nasty little truth about "making a living to pay the bills" rears its impish head only to ruin the dream.

My recent trip to Boston and Cape Ann has presented yet another post-vacation wrestling match. Not only have the beauty of cooler temps; rambling hills and ridiculously curvaceous roads; tight, old city streets and alleyways; houses that sit two stories in the front and four stories in the back, perched on wondrous precipices; and freshly-caught, thick slabs of halibut and haddock, not to mention the mutant-sized wriggling lobsters, all conspired to make this transition almost unbearable (since Central Florida contains absolutely none of the above mentioned joys), but the return to ***a geography depleted of trees*** has been one of the harshest realities to face (next comes the traffic on I-4, the problems, the routines, the expectations, and so on)!

New England was alive with magnificent flowers and oh so many trees. Amazed by the breathtaking scenery, I can see why so many poets and writers from the northeast celebrate trees in their writing. Unfortunately, here in Central Florida, trees seem to be treated more as nuisances (they might fall on someone's house in a storm), or worse yet, obstacles to "progress," i.e. another strip mall, gated community, or "luxury" apartment complex.

I experienced the beauty of trees of all kinds…rich green hues against the chiseled granite slopes and crystal blue skies—lush canopies that made music outside the windows of my cottage (which, by the way, were left open most of my stay) whenever the winds stirred and the sea-salted air rushed in from the nearby coves and harbor. The trees sang their rustling tunes as their branchy fingers took swipes against the window panes and bead-boarded exterior of the cottage.

Alas, in our part of the world, the propensity to cement and asphalt the land where mighty canopies of trees once stood seems quite criminal, when compared to the majesty of trees running amok in New England.

While pulling into the cramped parking lot of a tiny art gallery called "The Sacred Cod," as I was once again breathing in the pungent palette of greens and blues and cotton whites, I happened to notice a large, towering plant jutting up from the edge of the asphalted area. Right there, smack dab in the midst of the blackened shroud that covered the three car spaces, was a glorious milkweed plant, flowering at the top, ready to welcome a soon-to-be-passing by squadron of butterflies. Despite every attempt to cover over any signs of life—life was not to be denied! Here, in this stately milkweed, I witnessed an amazing truth about life—there is a power in new life that's strong enough to beat back every attempt at denying it a chance to thrive and blossom!

Those tiny seeds, germinating for who knows how long beneath that potent shield, finally mustered enough power to push through, breaking apart the mighty asphalt with its slender, yet stately stem. You and I would need a hammer and chisel and a good amount of sweat-equity to make so much as a dent in the parking lot surface, but here, this gracious plant, needed no tools other than those which are in its very nature as a plant—to reach up, to push out, to find its way to the sun, and to grow and blossom so that it might fulfill its purpose. Nothing would stand in its noble way. And the butterflies are grateful for that (as is the shop keeper, who gets to enjoy their daily visits during the summer months, as she paints canvases of beauty from the other side of the storefront window).

I'm not sure why this should have come as a surprise to me, this living thing breaking through all attempts to deny it abundance. After all, am I not part of a great multitude that claims belief in a Savior whom God raised from the dead, blowing open the mammoth seal rolled over the grave's entrance? For God, life is never to be denied—no matter its form or the degree of usefulness we choose to render it!

What we so often want to bury, to cover over with asphalt or cement…or with fear, bigotry, hatred, disinterest, jealousy, neglect, denial, convenience, or a host of other "sealants"…always seems to find a way to break through with a mighty force. Most often, we think we've done the deed, rid ourselves of the nuisances or obstacles. And then, imperceptibly at first, surely intending to catch us by surprise, what was buried springs back, bursts forth, and will not be denied. We may be amazed by its "sudden" appearance, and shocked to learn that its secret powers have surpassed all our efforts to keep it away. But truth be told, living things usually have a way of breaking through—and therein lays a potent hope for us all.

# THE STORY INSIDE:
## *ROLLING BACK THE STONE!*

Let me spread out the snapshots on the table...take a look and see what thread seems to be connecting them.

Here's the little boy running through the doorway, his breathing just short of needing a paper bag for hyperventilation. His eyes are bursting with a gleaming light that rivals Superman's laser vision. His gaping mouth betrays a tug-of-war between shouting and screaming. All the signs are there...something BIG has happened...and he simply can't hold it any longer.

This one finds the teenage girl sitting in the counselor's office, twisted and contorted like a pile of spaghetti, and just as hot, clutching her aching stomach, and rocking...rocking back and forth...which seems to now shake loose the tears. All the signs are there...something BIG has happened...and she simply can't get it out.

Finally, the dark, grainy one makes the shriveled skin and dark circles even more ominous. He's obviously been through life and back more times than he'd care to remember. In this one, he clutches the portrait of himself in his uniform—no, not the shiny one with all the medals, but rather the one with the stripes and the large number across his chest—his "yearbook" picture from Auschwitz. All the signs are there...something BIG has happened since those days...but will anyone care to hear an old, broken, and barely audible man's story yet another time?

Maya Angelou once wrote: ***"There is no greater agony than bearing an untold story inside you."***

This "agony" can taste like the flavor of great joy, ready to burst our heart and skin for the sheer power of it in our lives. Something beautiful and wonderful happens to us; we achieve something that's been the result of incredible commitment, or perhaps the surprising fortune of being at the right place at the right time. Either way, this untold story pounds on the roof of our mouth and begs to be shared.

This "agony" can also taste like a damp, dark jail cell, where the story has been imprisoned out of fear of retribution, or embarrassment, or shame, or guilt, or unspeakable pain. Like any prisoner, this story longs for freedom and fresh air, but the sentence has been passed, and the inner laws one has created must be obeyed. Yet, it is a story that yearns to be unshackled.

This "agony" can bear the stripes of the public or private evils that cut to the core of humanity, that tear at the very fabric of civilization; the horror of this agony can become so unspeakable that persons and nations and cultures feverishly try to bury or deny the horror. Yet, as Angelou so rightly asserts, the untold, unredeemed story must break forth against all odds—if in fact, redemption is to have a chance to shine.

Every moment of every day, we all bear stories within us that yearn for a telling. But they are so deep, so personal, and so full of vulnerability that we become accustomed to hiding and protecting them from anyone—lest we suffer the greater indignities we believe will flow from their telling. And so we suffer, and we weep, and "unknown" rumblings trouble us in our souls, and we turn to palliatives to mask the pain...but the stories refuse to go away.

But when the opening comes, when the relationship with another is strong and trustworthy enough, when the taste of freedom is sweeter than the dread of concealment, when the stone is finally rolled away in spite of the "stench" that may temporarily linger—resurrection is possible and life can begin anew!

On the road to Emmaus, so poignantly rendered for us by the Evangelist Luke, the unnamed disciples, who sound suspiciously like us in our sometimes-despondent wanderings, experience the resurrected Lord Jesus only after their painful story breaks forth from their souls. In the course of their wayward journey, a stranger joins them who provided a safe place, an oasis of freshness wherein they felt courageous enough to unleash the agony inside them: "we had desperately, perhaps foolishly hoped he was the one!" This story of profound hurt and pain and guilt had been pleading for release since the apparent defeat of the crucifixion, and the cowardly desertion by Jesus' disciples. But like so many stories that find refuge in the deepest places of ourselves, there was no one to trust with this hauntingly personal story, no one who could hold it and caress it (the way Jesus must have gently caressed the feet of these same disciples at the Last Supper) with the tenderness and understanding it deserved.

That is...until the risen Lord appeared in their midst... and he allowed them to tell their story first! And as it had been throughout Jesus' entire life, once again, the journey to Emmaus was *first* about *them*, and only secondly about him. Once their story was set free, Jesus began to breathe new life into them by gathering up the tattered shreds of their story into the GREAT STORY of God and God's ultimate victory over death. Stories of seeming death were revisited...and the seeds of new life were found just beneath the surface. Watered by the tears that so often accompany an untold story, the seeds of life begin to sprout.

In this grand season of new life, this Easter of God, are there story-stones that need rolling back in our lives, stories whose *agony* we can no longer confine—whether the agony be that of a joy we've failed to share because we thought no one would care to listen, or whether the agony be that of a deep sorrow we've failed to share for the same reason.

The risen Lord Jesus is alive and amongst us, and God continues to roll back stones of death so that stories of life might come forth!

# JESUS THE STRANGER

## "The Right Reverend Stronger"
## by Tom Furlong

*If I believe*
*Who I receive*
*at aisle's end*
*is both my Saviour*
*and my friend*
*then I'll treat*
*the stranger*
*in the street*
*as I do*
*the priest*
*who hands*
*the Eucharist*
*to me.*

Listening in on the edge of a conversation not so long ago, I was fascinated with the way in which one of the people in the group was attempting to describe someone he met on a recent business trip. The other members of the group paid close attention as he stretched and grabbed at innumerable adjectives to illuminate this particular individual. Finally, in a fit of exasperation, seemingly unable to adequately capture the person he met, he blurted out in no uncertain and clearly definitive terms: "He was just 'strange'!"

Everyone kind of chuckled, and then quickly turned their attention away from the unknown "strange" one and back to the fine vintage of Merlot they were sipping. Ever wonder if anyone has ever described you as "strange"? I suppose we would be highly offended precisely because we spend a good bit of our lives trying not to say or do anything that might be construed as "strange" by anyone. We have a general tendency to want to fit in, to not make waves, to appear "normal," and to come across as regular as the summer rains on a Florida afternoon.

Isn't it fascinating then that as we celebrate the resurrection appearances of Jesus throughout the 50 days of this great Paschal Season, it's clear that the resurrected Jesus is not easily described nor recognized. In fact, although the scriptures do not use the exact word, it is not too much of a leap of imagination to hear the apostles and disciples summarizing their encounter with the risen Lord as "strange!" Jesus, who had been friend, companion, confidant, mentor, prophet, teacher, Lord and Master; Jesus, the one who created the ultimate bond of intimacy between himself and his followers by offering them his very Body and Blood—food and drink unto eternal life—is now STRANGER—the unrecognized, questionable, mysterious, perplexing, and incomprehensible one.

What happened to him in the resurrection that caused his closest friends to question his identity, to have the urgent need to press his wounded hands, feet and side, to mistake him for a ghost, or gardener, or uninformed pilgrim? How was it possible that the very Jesus—with whom they had eaten and slept, had traveled and taught, had spent countless hours listening to the lilt of his voice and watching the contours of his face change from joy to sadness, from anguish to anger, from rejoicing to resignation—had now become a stranger to them?

Perhaps, Jesus "became" someone he always instructed his followers to never forget—the stranger! The risen Jesus as "stranger" now fully embodied the prodigal son, the woman at the well, the leper who cried out for mercy, the nameless maimed one along the roadside to Jericho, the ranting and raving possessed lunatic breaking chains. Perhaps in his resurrected body, he wanted to remind his disciples never to judge simply by first impressions or mere appearances. Perhaps he intended to leave them with the indelible command to be fully present and attentive to the people they would meet as they went about proclaiming the Good News—seeing them as God sees them and not with the eyes of the world. Perhaps it was the simple confirmation that Jesus as "Stranger" would be a piece of the testimony and experience of every follower of Christ down through the ages, as each of us struggles with the meaning of Jesus in our lives. Perhaps the power of "the One who comes to us as 'Stranger'" reminds us of the always mysterious and unsettling ways in which God approaches us, so that we might never lose sight of who alone is the author of our lives.

From our vantage point in time and history, it seems almost unfathomable to grasp the intensity of those first encounters with the resurrected Lord Jesus by his apostles and disciples—that incredible mixture of fear and festivity, hurt and healing, dreaminess and rapture. Yet, in the midst of all the "strangeness," one thing is ever so clear and loudly proclaimed by the testimonies of those who experienced the risen Lord Jesus—HE IS TRULY ALIVE! And "alive" in tangible and palpable ways—not merely in some hopeful reminiscence, restless desire, or wild imaginative fantasy.

This resurrected Lord and Savior is still very much alive in our midst, still very much the compassion of God drawing us to the Father. Yet, not unlike the experiences of those first astonished and awestruck disciples, we still wrestle with Jesus' "strangeness." Despite all our efforts at times to tame him, to box him in, to handle him according to our plans and projects, to let him be only what we think we want or need him to be for us, to organize and control him and his Good News—this Jesus continues to break loose of our bondage just as he broke loose from the bonds of his funeral wrappings and the stone-sealed tomb. And although we still find him "strange," or we even overlook his presence in our midst because he appears as the "stranger" we want to shun or avoid, he still comes to us calling our names, offering us peace and the gifts of the Holy Spirit, and inviting us into the fullness of life—until we fully awaken, recognize and embrace him.

# SPRINGTIME

*In Lewis Carroll's "Through the Looking Glass," an enlightening conversation takes place between little Alice, who tumbled into "Wonderland," and the Queen: "'There's no use, trying,' Alice said; 'one can't believe impossible things.'*

*'I dare say you haven't had much practice,' said the Queen. 'When I was your age, I always did it for half-an-hour a day. Why, sometimes, I've believed as many as six impossible things before breakfast....'"*

*Springtime is an invitation to believe as many "impossible" things as our hearts desire...whether before breakfast, or at the close of a long day!*

# THE FIRST GREAT "HANDING OVER": *A TRIP TO DOWNTOWN PITTSBURGH*

I remember the excitement and enthusiasm as I prepared for my first trip by bus into downtown Pittsburgh with my friends from the neighborhood. Sure, I had been there several times before with my parents or with my grandmother, but now I was finally old enough, mature enough to spend the day in the company of my friends roaming the streets of the city!

Long before the required permission was granted, or even broached, my friends and I had the whole day's itinerary worked out. At the time, we were all into model rocketry and the related science of smoke bomb manufacturing! (I must be honest in saying that our rocket launches were much more successful than our attempts at creating fireworks). Consequently, our first trek after arrival on 5th Avenue was to Fisher Scientific, where a small hobby shop would provide all the necessary equipment required for our experiments. At our ages, we weren't interested in shopping for clothes, so there was little concern for stops at Kaufmann's, Horne's, or Gimbel's Department stores (except, perhaps, for a few rides on the escalators—going backwards, of course!). Lunch options were a key consideration...always a tossup between the lunch counter at Woolworth or McCrory's (RIP), or the humongous "Oyster House" fish sandwich, the kind which left you with a bad case of lock-jaw following the first bite. If there were to be time to spare after all this, a visit to Honus Wagner's Sports Store was in order, giving us the opportunity to lust after authentic Pittsburgh Pirate sports gear and collectibles.

Yes indeed, the itinerary planning provided many hours of enjoyment, as we mapped it all out during idle hours while perched on the front balcony of our clubhouse nestled in the woods, or during breaks from our scientific work while gathered around the mock-up chemistry labs we created in our basements or garages. The dreaming was fun…the mustering up of enough *gumption*, as Russell Baker calls it, to ask permission—now that was another story!

Asking permission was a little frightening at first, but when the long awaited "yes" came from my parents' lips, I felt that a great *responsibility* was being HANDED OVER to me. I think it is safe to say, without exaggeration, that I was in as much awe as any 11 year old is capable of. I recall how proud I was, but at the same time, I was nervous; I was both glad and afraid (although, I would never have let on to my friends that I was experiencing the latter of the two emotions).

When the glorious day of departure finally arrived, as the bus pulled up to the stop, right in front of my house, I remember looking back and seeing my grandmother looking through the lacy curtains of the kitchen window. When she saw that I was looking, my grandma quickly ducked out of sight. She didn't want me to know that she, too, was proud and nervous, glad and afraid.

Perhaps each of us can recall moments when others who have been responsible *for* us or responsible *to* us make *us* responsible for ourselves. We experienced that sense of joy that comes with being allowed to do something on one's own for the first time—a great commission; the relaying of an important message; undertaking a special task; or simply being old enough to venture into the city as a young boy of 11.

As we approach the Feast of the Ascension and the impending culmination of the Easter Season, if we have been at all attentive to the invitations extended through our scripture proclamations, we have heard and witnessed Jesus beginning to HAND OVER responsibility to his disciples. Sure, he had been sending them out during the three years of his itinerant preaching and healing ministry, but they had always been able to come back, to sit down at his feet, listen to his counsel and encouragement, and feel the total security that came with resting in his presence. Sure, they had shared some responsibility along the path of his public ministry, but now that responsibility was growing by leaps and bounds. Jesus was to be with them only a short time longer. We hear him say in the scriptures: "A little while, and I will be with you no longer; a little while, and you will be alone; a little while, and you will be independent; a little while, and you will have to stand on your own feet!"

My suspicion is that unlike the surge of enthusiasm with which I embraced my anxiously awaited day of running around all the hot spots of downtown Pittsburgh solely in the company of my boyhood companions, the disciples were not looking forward to their day of "growing up" with the same reckless abandon! They had witnessed the cost of the kind of responsibility Jesus was about to entrust to them—and it was surely frightening!

From the moment that we were first initiated into the Body of Christ, we, too, have been entrusted with responsibility. It has grown and developed, and it has taken on a heavier cost as we have grown in age and life experience. Perhaps we have, at various stages of our own life of faith, grasped this responsibility with less than enthusiastic commitment, or perhaps we have had the sense that maybe we're "not ready" or "old enough" to handle what is required!

Jesus has given us a great responsibility...he has handed over his mission of spreading the Good News of God to us. It is a wonderful responsibility...full of life, joy, exhilaration, and challenge. If we truly embraced the mission and ministry that have been entrusted to us, then we would experience, with more certainty and celebration, the power of God alive in our world. Whether through the pages of sacred scripture, or through the stories of people's lives in our own community, those who have willingly accepted Jesus' handing on of responsibility have experienced the power to do great things in his name: unclean spirits have been cast out, paralytics and cripples have been cured, ordinary people have been roused to acts of compassion and the desire (and ability) to make real and lasting changes in their lives.

Once this responsibility for carrying on the Good News of God is embraced with enthusiasm and commitment, GREAT THINGS begin to happen. If you're not convinced or cling to a cynical view of what is capable through the power of faith in God, there are plenty of people within arm's reach every Sunday, within arm's reach while you are at work, or school, or play, who can give testimony to this fact! Just ask one of the newly initiated into our community...spend a moment with someone recovering from the loss of a spouse, or home, or loved one...listen to the quiet prayer of the lonely figure kneeing before the Blessed Sacrament…hear the praise and thanksgiving lifted after an experience of physical, emotional or spiritual healing…look into the eyes of a hospital or nursing home patient who has just received the holy anointing of the Church and see the comfort and peace that often illuminate his or her face.

Yes, great things happen when the responsibility of

faith takes root, but the responsibility that has been handed over to us, as we know all too well, can be frightening—even when it brings about Good News! Instead of joy and exhilaration, we can experience frustration, despair, and anxiety.

As the day of Pentecost draws near, let us take courage and strength from Jesus' promise...the promise of a Paraclete...a Comforter. Jesus tells us, I will not leave you orphaned. I will give you another helper—the Holy Spirit. It is the Spirit of the Living God who dwells within each of us…stirring us to acts of compassion, wiping away our despair, propelling us forward into the corners of life where the peace of Christ is desperately needed, reminding us of God's constant love and care.

I recall returning from that maiden voyage to downtown Pittsburgh filled with a spirit of honor, trust, enthusiasm, exhilaration and pride. I had not disappointed my parents on the occasion of this great "handing over"; consequently, there were to be many such days that followed in the years ahead.

Filled with the Spirit of the Paraclete, the great Fire of God alive in our hearts, can we go forth into each day of our lives with any less enthusiasm and exhilaration?

# THOSE IN-BETWEEN DAYS

Days of waiting can be exciting, if we are anticipating something enjoyable and happy: birthdays, graduations, weddings, and the return of someone we love. But **"in-between" days**, waiting days can be filled with fear, worry, uncertainty and questions. Sometimes, those in-between days, those waiting days are the hardest to pass through. I recall what have been, to date, my hardest "waiting, in-between" days—the days spent at my grandmother's hospital bedside before she died. Those kinds of days, as many have experienced, are perhaps the most prolonged days of one's life. There is nothing else to do but wait—to await the inevitable—and to prepare. But we never really seem to be able to prepare very well, since the inevitable event brings with it its own drama. Our normal, yet guilt-tinged feelings, which bubble to the surface in those in-between times, usually center on one prayer: *Please God, let it be over soon!*

It seems that the hardest part of being in-between, of waiting is that we are saying someone or something else is *in control.* We do not have all the power in our hands to do what we want or need; we have to admit that many events and situations are *beyond our control*, and we have to be patient and trusting, even when that seems impossible.

The Seventh Sunday of Easter always strikes me as an in-between Sunday. In many ways, we are, as Christians, an in-between people. We are, like the apostles and followers of Jesus, gathered in the upper room after the Ascension—we are in-between and waiting.

The apostles were afraid, uncertain, wondering what was next. They oscillated between two questions: *Is this the end? Or is this just a pause, an intermission before we get on with our mission?*

This past week, we celebrated the Feast of the Ascension, with the apostles left "looking up into the sky." Next Sunday, we celebrate the Feast of Pentecost, the sending of the Holy Spirit. But *this* week, we are in-between, waiting like the apostles.

What do we do in these in-between days? Hide? Give up? Go about "business as usual" (as if we have never heard the God News)? Have doubts?

Or, do we respond like the apostles and **pray**...pray constantly for the power of the Holy Spirit to come into our lives?

*The Spirit will come*…Jesus promises this! We are waiting...but the Spirit of God will come. Are we in need of the Spirit? Do we want the Spirit?

**Yes, we need the fire of the Spirit!** There is pain,

suffering, fear, doubt, anger, jealousy; hence, there is healing that needs to take place. We need to have the fire of God's love and the power of the Good News stirred up again—the flame is getting low.

Jesus came into the world so that we "might have life and have it to the full." We may be in-between; we may be waiting, but let's not stand with our heads in the clouds. Let us pray, with all the faith we can muster; let us pray for the Spirit of God to descend like a flame into our hearts and the heart of our community.

# "HOW 'BOUT A LITTLE FIRE, SCARECROW?!"

Sitting in a basement game room (my apologies to all life-long Floridians who cannot relate to a "basement) as a child, watching the ***Wizard of Oz***, was an exhilarating, albeit frightening experience. There were all manner of creepy and "off limits" nooks and crannies in that game room. My dad's workshop was definitely not the place to play, although my brother and sister and I managed to find our way in there on occasion (and suffered the consequences of that ill-fated decision). Then there was the "oil tank room," simply hidden behind a louvered door, where the fuel was stored to run the furnace. We were convinced that this was nothing more than a facade for the opening to hell! Our childhood imaginations often ran wild as to the beasts and monsters that lived in that room, and surely were licking their chops waiting for one of us to venture in—never to be seen again. I'm sure my brother and I threatened to lock my sister in there if she didn't cooperate with one of our usual schemes to eat her candy or to get her to do our chores.

So, it's an easy stretch of the imagination to realize that watching the *Wizard of Oz* in this setting made for high drama. I loved the *Wizard of Oz*, and still do, but I hated the witch! Looking at her now, she seems quite comical with her overdone, colorized green face and large wart. But back then, there was nothing comical about her—she was deadly frightening. I wouldn't have been surprised if she had popped out of the "oil tank room" one night while we were watching TV. In fact, I used to think I could hear her voice coming from behind the louvered door: "I'll get you, my little pretty!"

Watching all of her mean and nasty antics throughout the story, the one scene that troubled me most (although those hideous flying monkeys run a close second) was her vicious tossing of a fire-ball at the Scarecrow, setting him ablaze. In her scratchy, irritating and devious voice, she asks: "How 'bout a little fire, Scarecrow?"

While there weren't any witches with sickly green faces and wart-tipped noses in the Upper Room at the first Pentecost, I wonder whether the men and women gathered there that day would have been thrilled had Jesus warned them ahead of time that when the Holy Spirit comes, there's going to be FIRE—and it's going to rest on top of your heads! Perhaps we have a rather benign image of this event due to much of the overly pious religious art that depicts the Descent of the Holy Spirit. By now, we probably yawn when hearing the Acts account of the "tongues of fire" or seeing the little wisps of flame dancing atop the disciples' heads.

But stop and think about it—it's FIRE! It's hot ... it's got a mind of its own ... it can be destructive… it burns... it is unpredictable...it's dangerous! Can you image the look on the disciples' faces if Jesus had said to them: "How 'bout a little fire, Peter ...or James...or Mary...or Martha?"

There is incredible intensity about fire that we fear; we have seen its dangers and destruction. We have witnessed vast forests felled by raging infernos; we have seen people's lives torn apart and have watched them gently clinging to charred pieces of life-long memories after their homes have been ravaged by fire; we've learned from an early age, "play with fire and you get burned!" And it is precisely because of this very INTENSITY that the Holy Spirit is depicted, in one of her many forms, as coming in FIRE!

As we make our way post-Pentecost, I wonder what our response to Jesus would be if he were to ask us directly, "How 'bout a little fire?" Do we want the FIRE of the Holy Spirit, or are we more comfortable with the Spirit as "gentle dove," casually floating above our world and us? Perhaps we find the Spirit as "gentle breeze" less threatening and more soothing, much like the soft wind off the lake on a beautiful Spring evening. But FIRE... how can we abide with the havoc the Spirit stirs up when bursting upon our Church and us like a blazing fire?

Jesus desired just that, a Church set on fire by his preaching and ministry, a world infused with the flame of the Spirit, a baptism that truly transforms lives and sets people ablaze, when in Luke's Gospel we find: "I came to bring fire to the earth, and how I wish it were already kindled! I have a baptism with which to be baptized, and what stress I am under until it is completed! (12:49-50)"

Perhaps these harsh words of Jesus are not appealing to us, and we have our ways of toning them down. We still may be frightened by the threat of "fire," but not from some fantasy character with an ugly green face in a child's tale, but rather by the gift of the enduring, abiding presence of the Lord Jesus Christ, through his Holy Spirit. But without the fire, we are lost. Without the fire, the Church becomes just one more institution in a long history of laws, and structures and broken promises, which claim the allegiance and faith of people, only to disappoint and leave them unfulfilled.

The great English Romantic poet, William Blake, who touched on many visionary spiritual themes in his writing, once penned these words, words we might take to heart:

*Unless the eye catch fire, God will not be seen.*
*Unless the ear catch fire, God will not be heard.*
*Unless the tongue catch fire, God will not be named.*
*Unless the heart catch fire, God will not be loved.*
*Unless the mind catch fire, God will not be known.*

Unless WE catch fire, is it any wonder that our world still does not know the grace and peace of Our Lord, Jesus Christ?!

# SOMETIMES A MIGHTY WIND, SOMETIMES A GENTLE BREATH

"Change" is a perplexing thing—especially *personal* change. We all know how hard it is, and sometimes I wonder why it takes a major personal catastrophe (and then, sometimes, even that doesn't work) for any of us to institute new steps in our lives. I keep thinking that there are things I'd like to change, but gee, do I really have to wait until I am diagnosed with heart disease, or cancer, or perhaps experience the loss of someone important in my life, in order for me to muster the energy and resolve to make the changes I desire?

A couple of weeks ago, as I was reflecting on the powerful scriptures for the Feast of Pentecost, I was immediately touched by the glaring contrast in the depictions of the "arrival" of the Holy Spirit as recounted by Luke in the Acts of the Apostles and the Evangelist John. In Acts, we find the story unfolding this way: "And suddenly there came from the sky a noise like ***a strong driving wind,*** and it filled the entire house in which they were...and they were filled with the Holy Spirit (2:2-4)."

However, another account of the giving of the Holy Spirit strikes a completely different chord, as we read in John's gospel: "Jesus said to them again, `Peace be with you. As the Father has sent me, so I send you.' And when he had said this, ***he breathed on them*** and said to them, `Receive the Holy Spirit' (20:21-22)."

Now which is it? Is it the "strong driving wind" swirling about the Upper Room, or is it the gentle "breath" of a newly risen Christ that confers the magnificent gifts of the Holy Spirit upon beleaguered disciples?

As I began to think about it, I came to realize: sometimes it takes a mighty wind, and sometimes it takes a gentle breath to move us off center, and to inaugurate the sweeping and subtle changes we desire in our lives and in our world.

While the more dramatic "winds" seem to get the attention, there are many gentle breaths that blow in our lives and bring us to the edge of reformation. I recall an experience when someone once told me that they began their career, really their "vocation" to serve the needs of the poor in Brazil simply by watching a 10 minute video that a friend had taken while on a trip into the remote, impoverished jungles there. Now I am sure that perhaps there had been other "stirrings" in their life at one time or another that may have lead to the "video-revelation," but to hear her speak about it, there were no flashes of lightning, no life-threatening diseases, and no financial collapses. Simply that video, and an open heart that was willing to truly take in what she was visually witnessing, provided all the flame she needed to ignite a marvelous journey of service and personal fulfillment.

I think about times of frustration throughout my college teaching career, when I went home at the end of many days wondering what in the world I was doing in a classroom filled with students who were forced to take courses in religion, and often had no more interest in the subject at hand than they did in getting a root canal! And often, in the midst of this debilitating attitude and outlook, when I was on the verge of simply "going through the motions" at each class meeting (much like I felt the students were doing), a gentle breath would touch my spirit, as someone would step forward and share with me the impact my class was having on their life (not simply their GPA). Often it was just that simple "breath," and not some "mighty wind," or new teaching skill, or monumental revelation, or salary raise that moved me off center (or should I say, up and out of the pit) and helped nudge me on to make the attitude adjustment, and to reinvest in my call to teaching.

The difficulty seems to be that these "breaths" are hard to catch. In the midst of challenge and depression, in the midst of failing commitments and depleted energies, we want to look for mighty winds to set us in a new direction, and we miss the subtlety of a gentle breath. In the middle of our wrestling match with despondency, it's hard to pick up on something as unspectacular as a comment, a kindness, a good wish, a sunset, a letter, a rainbow, or a smile. The Spirit is indeed being offered and rendered to us, but in our being overwhelmed (or perhaps being "under-whelmed"), we miss the nudge.

Yet, I am also aware that sometimes, in the midst of the challenges and both the need and desire for change, a gentle breath is not sufficient, that indeed it takes more, much more, something along the lines of a "strong, driving wind."

The Pentecost scriptures seem to strike a balance between the rush of a force and the quietness of a touch. Sometimes, the gentle breath is too subtle for where we happen to be. It may not carry the energy and dynamism that is necessary for us to get up and get moving. There are clearly times in our lives when the only voice we'll heed is the one that speaks louder and longer than our own voice, filled with excuses, concessions and compromises. This is not to say, however, that when we seem to really be stuck and unable to change our deep-seated attitudes, behaviors, or practices, we should get down on our knees and plead for a disaster to strike us. Rather, experience tells us that in fact events and experiences occur in our lives that jolt and rattle us to such a degree that we are forced to at least *pay attention*, if not to ultimately make changes. On occasion, it proves to be true that some of the larger-than-life train wrecks of our lives are actually the result of our having missed or having refused to act upon a series of opportunities for change. We shake our heads and say things like, "if only I had known (when in fact we really did know)," or perhaps "if only I had listened to my heart the first and second time I felt this way (but for many reasons, we did not listen)."

We are not always the best judges of which approach works best for us in any given situation: the mighty wind or the gentle breath. God moves in our lives in a variety of ways, and the Spirit's prompting and/or pushing can come from any angle or corner of our lives. The Spirit is indeed wild and untamable, and the Spirit of Jesus Christ seems to know which method is needed in trying to open us to new experiences and depths of living.

Sometimes...it takes a mighty wind...and sometimes... it takes a gentle breath. Is either blowing in your life right now?

# THE HOLY SPIRIT— UP CLOSE AND PERSONAL

Several years ago, I had the opportunity to make a return visit to one of the true wonders of North America—Niagara Falls. My very first trek to the Falls came near the end of my 8$^{th}$ grade year in elementary school. While most 8$^{th}$ grade classes prior to mine made their annual class trips to places like Washington, DC, Philadelphia, or some other "educational" locale, my class decided that these places were far too boring! Rather than waste our hard-earned class treasury, garnered over the course of the year from our Bingo nights and Christmas tree sales, on seeing yet another historical battle field or museum, my classmates and I got adventurous and set our sights on Niagara Falls (Canadian side, of course)!

As we were thinking about "exotic" destinations to which we could travel as our final act as the Class of 1972 (of course, these "exotic" sights had to been within a one-day round trip drive from Pittsburgh), many of us discovered that our parents had celebrated their honeymoons at the Falls. However, we did not end up choosing the trip for romantically nostalgic purposes—but we figured with those wonderful memories still planted in our parents' minds and hearts, they'd surely give us permission to make such a journey—and they did! Thinking back on it now, I can't imagine how we ever convinced Sister Bernadette, our Dominican principal, to allow for this expedition. Perhaps she was a great fan of natural beauty and justified our trip as a "geographic" adventure. Whatever the justifications, we just played along. Most of us boys were only interested in the fact that, upon crossing the Canadian border, we'd be able to get access to one of the most coveted (and totally illegal in Pennsylvania) possessions any 8$^{th}$ grade male could get his grimy hands on—FIREWORKS!

I had not returned to Niagara Falls since those heady days of fireworks and puppy love cuddling on the bus ride home from Canada. This latest trip, although devoid of contraband fireworks (now the contraband of interest was Cuban cigars), was exhilarating. The Falls of Niagara are stunning—the sheer power and glory of that never-ending, cascading water—is mesmerizing. I could park myself on a bench and stare at this awesome wonder for days on end. The famed "Maid of the Mist" boats still cruise below the Falls, filled with plastic-garbage-bag-clad tourists who, despite the cover-ups, still get a good dousing with water.

There's only one problem with this powerful wonder

of the world—**you can't really get close enough to it** to truly experience its awe! Somehow, simply looking at, observing, or taking pictures of these mighty waters leave me wanting more. Somehow, I fantasize about being a part of them—harnessing their powers, riding their billows and cascades, pounding the rocks below, having that sense of being driven over the edge with conviction and force!

Somehow…simply "looking" at this grand force of energy and beauty from an observation platform doesn't quite cut it for me.

However, I do know that some folks are quite content to "observe" this wonder from some point of safety and security. My aunt Becky is one of them! Once while on a trip to Niagara with my parents, she insisted that she could fully see and enjoy the Falls from the comfy confines of my parents' car parked along the side of the road! While we all knew that she simply didn't want the wind and water to mess up her hair-do, it seemed ridiculous to contend, as she stubbornly declared, that watching from a distance (behind the closed doors and windows of an automobile) was just as satisfying as riding the Maid of the Mist, or standing in the hollow cave openings behind the massive wall of cascading water!

I am moved to recall this contrast between myself and people like my aunt Becky, not to make a case for a summer trip to Niagara Falls, but rather because I see a parallel between this experience and the way some people approach the great wonder and mystery of the awesome gift of Christ to the Church, the "promise of the Father" which Jesus released upon his apostles and disciples—THE HOLY SPIRIT!

For some, the presence of the Holy Spirit, the beauty and power and grace that cascades from the heart of God, and is now the living presence of the Christ in our midst, is best left at a distance—to be looked upon, or observed, or timidly recited as the words in a half-spent prayer or hymn. For some, life in the Church is best left at a distance—to be admired as "a nice comfort to have in life," or perhaps to be an "ace in the hole" in case of disaster, or simply to be salve for an occasionally guilty conscience. For some, like my aunt Becky, it's better to stay behind protective covering when it comes to witnessing the works of the Spirit.

And yet, the Holy Spirit is given to all God's creation as the power by which the world is gradually transformed into the fullness of God's reign. The Holy Spirit is given not for show, or for looks, or for decoration—but rather to be USED, to be ENCOUNTERED, and to be both grabbed hold of and to be grabbed by! God desires us to be "up close and personal" with the Holy Spirit! The Spirit is meant to penetrate us, breaking through the obstacles we erect, knocking down the "observation platforms" we construct for safe viewing of the Spirit's work.

Nikos Kazantzakis in *The Saviours of God*, wrote: *The soul of man is a flame, a bird of fire that leaps from bough to bough, from head to head, and that shouts: 'I cannot stand still, I cannot be consumed, no one can quench me!'* It is the Holy Spirit of God, residing in our souls, who is this flame, this bird of fire leaping and bounding about! Such a Spirit cannot be quenched, or tamed, or merely "observed" from afar.

May this Pentecost find us drawing closer to the awesome power and grace of the Holy Spirit—getting up close and personal—rather than keeping our distance.

# RETURNING TO THE "SEAT OF LIFE," OUR MOTHER'S LAP

Long before President Woodrow Wilson declared "Mother's Day" a national holiday in 1915, we've been recognizing and celebrating "motherhood." Even as I pen this word, "motherhood," it strikes me now as being too static, too much of a cardboard cut-out term, smacking of a frozen set of letters calligraphied across the cover of a Hallmark greeting card. Better for us to speak of and reflect upon the *action* of being a mother, "mothering." (After all, we are all called to "mothering" in some way; it is not a gift limited only to a biological relationship... but more on that later.) Perhaps no other reality has been more discussed, debated, reflected upon, struggled with, and artistically presented, than mothering.

Some of the earliest sculptures created in human history give form and shape to the values embedded in mothering. Recently, while reviewing a delightfully challenging reflection on the nature of the Church by Sally Cunneen entitled, *Mother Church*, I came across her discussion of a particular type of sculpture of mothering that has been resurrected in countless forms throughout history — the "woman chair" sculpture. The creation of these sculptures stretches back to a most ancient depiction of the "Mother Goddess." In these sculptures, *the goddess is a woman whose lap, unnaturally extended, becomes a chair. She is literally the seat of life and growth*... The *lap* or *seat* becomes the symbolic center from which life not only flows, but to which it returns for nurturing. Cunneen describes the *lap* of mothering as a *holding environment— the space in which growth is fostered.*

What a powerful image of mothering; what a powerful image to pull out from our own storehouse of memory and to bring to life once again as a spark to ignite our reflection. Before consuming these remaining words, spend a few moments playfully musing in your mind's eye about the safety, security, warmth, nurturing, support, and gentleness you have experienced while cradled in a mother's lap....

I've turned the pages of albums and thumbed through faded photographs of my infancy, and I've been captured by the contentment that radiates from my face as I rest in my mother's lap, experiencing the satisfaction of her feeding, the stimulation of her smiling and laughing, the cooing of her soothing voice, the gentle stroking of her fingers over my head and face.

There are memories of returning to that holy space, after the days of infancy had long faded. The memories of running back after being on the receiving end of a demeaning barrage of ridicule from other children; memories of sheepishly cuddling up in that place after being punished for some misbehavior and then being invited to return for reconciliation; memories of dreamily pausing there to imagine my future life; memories of the initial disappointment when I reached the stage of growth where I thought I was too "big" (physically and emotionally) to seek out the comfort of my mother's lap; memories of resting my head there after crying the painful tears shed at my much beloved grandmother's death.

The image is even more potent when not only we are the ones who have been nestling in this sacred space, but the ones who have also offered our own laps for the nurturing of someone we love.

The sacred space of a mother's lap is a place in which we never seem to tire of resting, a holy place we long to return to throughout our lives. My mother and I have often joked throughout my "adult" years about her constant invitation, while home on vacations and holidays, to spend a few moments with her in a rocking chair. No...not a two-seater. Her offer is to *rock me* in that rocking chair! We do the dialogue routine every so often—she makes the offer, and I remind her of the serious injury that might occur if we were to give it a try—not to mention the sure and certain damage that would befall the family rocking chair! Now, I've seen my dad do some impressive "fixing" in his day—but this encounter would be irreparable!

Despite our concern over these health and safety issues, my mother's invitation to return to that sacred space of life-giving nourishment is always tempting. Leaving the rocker aside, we find other ways to express that closeness, that nurturing, that physical presence that is essential to each of our lives.

Of the many qualities that sustain one in mothering, perhaps the most significant, the most cherished (and the one most mourned when it is lost or physically inhibited in some way) is the ability to give life out of one's body. Whether through the great miracle of physical birthing or through the myriad symbolic ways in which each of us "gives life" through our bodies, we are invited into the creative work of God, the ultimate Giver-of-Life, and we are given a share in the Divine Creator's desire and ability to *renew* life in spite of the constant and natural rhythm of decay and death. This is true "mother-power" bestowed by the Creator—a power we are all asked to exercise throughout our lives.

The sacred space of a mother's lap, the sacred space from which we literally emanate and to which we seek to return to be rejuvenated, is blessed as a *holding environment.* It is the place where we can get our bearings after being disoriented or thrown into a tailspin by some experience of life; it is a locus of healing through the power of physical touch; it is a place with boundaries, which enables us to regroup when we have fallen into the boundary-shattering experiences of life, the ones we call *chaos*; it is a place of "resurrection" in the sense that we often emerge from this space, after having come face to face with the darkness of our tomb, with the light of a new day, with the glow of a new beginning.

As Sally Cunneen points out, it is in this same spirit that the ancient symbol of *Mother Church* arises. The image of *Mother Church,* depicted and characterized in a variety of ways since the earliest days of Christianity, conveys the reality of the Church as a *holding environment*, as well as a sacred space to return to throughout the course of one's life journey—a place of compassion and care, of nurturing and refreshment.

However, the image of the Church as *mother*, as a *holding environment,* has been corrupted and distorted throughout our history. At different times and in different places, the nurturing and caring environment has been interpreted and played out in demeaning, controlling and abusive ways. Rather than a nurturing *holding* environment, the "mothering" of the Church has been more like a *stranglehold*, a vise-like grip that has allowed little room for growth. Often, *Mother Church* has been guilty of trying to preserve us as hapless, completely dependent children, rather than the *adult* children we have become, living our lives in freedom and responsibility.

The true mother, while struggling with the risks of allowing her child to leave the safe boundaries of her lap, knows that her child will never grow into the beautiful creation God has blessed her with unless she first lets him or her go, allows him or her to venture forth in freedom. There is a great chasm that stretches between *mother—ing* and *smother—ing!*

As I ponder many things this Mother's Day, I am grateful that the *seat of life* from which I have sprung has provided me with not only an understanding of the power and call to *mothering* in my own life, but also an image and foundation for understanding the power in the way I live and minister in the Church. My own mother's lap continues to be a source of nourishment, support, and care. I have learned from the safety of that sacred and holy space that each of us is called to be a *holding environment* for others, an environment wherein people can find refreshment and rejuvenation, an environment *into* which people can freely enter and *from* which they are free to go.

As I ponder what I have been graced to receive from my own mother, as well as from my maternal grandmother and my godmother, I am challenged to emulate these qualities in my own life, both personally and in my life of priestly ministry.

I give thanks and praise to God on this day for my own mother, my grandmothers and godmother, too, and I strive to hear and see the ways in which God is calling every community of faith to share in the ministry of *Mother* Church. What kind of a *holding environment* are we creating? Is there enough room for people in need to find support, nurturing compassion, and gentle care? Is the lap of our particular community a sacred place where people can be nourished in Word and Sacrament, where their growth is fostered? Are we a community that knows when to "cuddle up," and when to let go? Are we learning the skills of a *mothering church* so that we may invite people to be fed, but be ready to equip them as they are sent back on their way into our beautiful, yet troubled, world?

In tribute to our mothers...no matter who they are or where they may now be...let us spend some time resting in their laps, receiving from them the grace of renewed life despite the decay and death we constantly face.

# SUMMERTIME

*It seems that the heat and humidity, the sultry summer weather do things to our minds. We get a bit light-headed and start musing about all sorts of perplexities. Probably the reason all those pictures of big, southern wrap-around porches, populated with people simply rocking in their chairs and sipping iced tea, not saying a word to each other, seem to capture our imagination.*

*Even the seemingly inconsequential act of listening to a radio broadcast of a baseball game on the porch during a summer's night in late August can become an occasion of clearer insight, a true epiphany. Ah, summertime...a much needed Sabbath for us all!*

# GULF-SCAPADES...RANDOM OBSERVATIONS FROM LIDO KEY

It's the month of June and the taste of salt water and sunshine is getting closer, as I anticipate some vacation time in a couple of weeks. Before heading off to create new "escapades" at the Gulf of Mexico, allow me to share some random observations that I first penned a number of years ago while on vacation to Lido Key. Perhaps you may want to find your own spot of sand, take a nice umbrella-decked beverage in hand...and then...read on!

## SEA FOAM

Sea foam is a curious creation of the ocean tides. At times, it seems as if someone, after deciding to complete this week's laundry in the ocean currents, has loaded up with too much detergent! The foam is light and airy. I suppose, in a way, that sea foam is the Gulf Coast's answer to Texas tumbleweed. Its rolling mounds of bubbles toss and tumble along the water's edge, ambling aimlessly until they hit the shore and are driven in all directions by a humid, summer eve's sea breeze. Yet, it strikes me that these whimsical creations are brought into being from the **agitation** of the sea. Out of the traumatic movement of the waters eventually comes a creation that seems to suit no important purpose, fulfills no significant need. From the agitation of the sea come these mounds of fluffy fluid and air, eventually rolling into oblivion.

Sometimes the agitations that are stirred in the "waters" of our own lives, that erupt from within the "sea" of our own daily experiences, produce nothing more than whimsical, purposeless results. So often, the nervous, agitated, ponderous, distracting movement from within us, which at the time they are occurring, seem to us to be destined to produce momentous changes or disruptions in our lives, result in little more than fluffy tumbleweeds, eventually rolling their way into oblivion.

How patient are we during these periods of agitation? Can we be more trusting in God that the upsetting movements within us will not always produce dramatic, traumatic results?

## TINY BIRDS PECKING IN THE SAND

It is fascinating to observe the tiny birds that make their living pecking in the sand as the tides roll in and out. As the waters recede from the sands, the birds, streaking forward, quickly dig for their nourishment, plucking microscopic tidbits from beneath the sand. As the waters crash back into the shore, their nearly invisible legs, no thicker than match sticks, move in lightening quick rhythm as they scurry up shore for safety. Their time is spent in continuous chasing of the waves back and forth, waiting for the proper moment to race forward with the ebbing tide, pecking gently below the surface, trying to grab what they can before they have to run away again.

Sometimes it seems, as we chase our own nourishment, our own happiness, even our spiritual fulfillment, we are like these tiny, sand-probing birds. Our pace is frenetic; we are often frightened by the waves, the in and out movement of the world around us; we only seem to scratch the surface, barely gaining bits and pieces of what we really need to feed us.

How much our approach to the nourishment God can provide is like the feeding patterns of these tiny, fragile creatures!

## YES, THERE IS A DIFFERENCE IN SAND

A classic argument exists between the learned and the inexperienced beachcombers; in fact, it is the easiest way to tell the difference between someone "in the know" and a "pretender." Yes, there *are* different kinds of sand! Oh sure, on first glance anyone can see that there are differences in color, especially depending upon which coast one happens to be traversing. But to the observant beach stalker, no matter what sandy shoreline one sinks his or her feet into, one encounters different types of sandy surfaces. There's the soft, sinking wet sand that quickly envelopes one's toes, yet firm enough to keep one from being swallowed. There's the coarse, bristly sand, the kind that scratches the bottom of one's feet and heats up to scorching temperatures on cloudless summer days. There's the shell-ridden variety, the kind that creates a tortuous path like walking on broken eggshells or sharp pieces of glass strewn about the kitchen floor after dropping a jar. This sandy terrain calls for a keen eye, especially vigilant in search of errant pieces of shell that jut out from the surface, ready to make a good slice in one's foot. There's the smooth, creamy sand, just washed over by the tides, that appears silky to the touch. There's the swirling, striated sand, which the water leaves behind in signature-sweeps like the dunes of a desert ridge.

These various sand terrains are reminiscent of the various terrains that comprise the landscape of our daily living, the encounters we have with God's Spirit. Walking the "beach" that is our own life, we encounter a variety of textures and tones—such is the graciousness and whimsy of our loving God!

# A SPIRITUALITY OF BARE FEET

While my folks love to pull out tiny, embarrassing snippets from my childhood from time to time, mostly to entertain and amuse people in my parishes who aren't privy to the intricacies of my younger days, on the other hand, I prefer to keep these revelations to a minimum.

One such minor snapshot came to mind this week; one that is relatively harmless to let fly! My parents have told me that when I was a little child, I disdained walking in the grass with my bare feet. I hear the story told that when I was placed in the grass, on what I'm sure was a lovely spring or summer day, I would immediately curl up my toes—mistakenly assuming, I suppose, that this would protect me, as though I were a turtle drawing back into its shell! Quickly realizing that this tactic did little to quell my fears, I simply burst into a volley of tears!

When I hear this story, I often wonder whether this was something my mom and dad did in order to help me overcome my fears, or whether they simply enjoyed doing this—some form of kiddy torture for my misbehaving!

Fortunately, for them and for me, I eventually conquered my distaste for prickly blades of grass against my tender feet. (Although, later in childhood, I had to work my way through yet another "bare foot" scare—concern that my feet might become HUGE if I didn't wear shoes!)

Actually, it's better to say that not only did I conquer my fear, but that I came to greatly enjoy bare-footed romps through grass... and sandy beaches... and muddy fields. There's just something liberating, refreshing and spiritual about slipping out of the confinement of socks and shoes and frolicking closer to the ground. While clad in shoes, we somehow isolate ourselves from the earth, from the very primordial muck from which Genesis tells us we were fashioned by our Creator.

I recall my first trip to the Hawaiian Islands and the vast array of beauty that consumed me. As the lush, tropical world enveloped every ounce of my being, I began to experience how freeing it felt to be running around either barefoot or sporting only my flimsy sandals (or "slippers" as the islanders call them). The ability to soak in the beauty and relaxation that this tropical paradise afforded was not confined only to my senses of hearing, sight and smell. *Touch* was incredibly important—and my feet touching the ground enabled me to relax and to embrace the beauty of the lands and the peoples I encountered.

Recall that Moses, during his mountaintop theophany, was invited by the voice calling out from the burning bush to "take off his shoes." In a sense, before being allowed to enter into the realm of Yahweh, before encountering the Lord of Hosts, Moses had to first free himself of any encumbrances, obstacles that would hinder his welcome of God. Chucking his shoes was the tangible way in which he prepared himself to "stand on holy ground."

It seems that our own awareness of "holy ground" meets with many obstacles. A considerable amount of "un-holiness" is daily thrust upon us; our care for the environment continues to take a back seat to economic growth and development; in an age where we tell ourselves that we are finally freed from rigid Victorian sexual mores and now can embrace healthier relationships, the reality is that superficiality and violent abuse characterize many contemporary relationships; while we give voice to "spiritual" longings stirring in the depths of our souls, we are often slow to act upon those "stirrings" by entering into a community of faith, choosing instead to pursue God "on our own."

"Taking off our shoes," it can be said, is the beginning of spiritual growth, of deepening our encounters with God—the God who is manifested in creation, in humanity, in the sacramental life of the Church. And, taking off our shoes is not a one-time act of submission, but rather it is an on-going ritual in which to engage.

Macrina Wiederkehr in *Seasons of Your Heart* puts it this way:

## FIRESTARTERS

*Taking off shoes is a sacred ritual. It is a hallowed moment, a way of celebrating the holy ground on which you stand. Whether you take off your shoes symbolically or literally matters little. What is important is that you are alive to the holy ground on which you stand and to the holy ground that you are.*

Not unlike my toddler phobia of bare feet in the grass, we continue to experience a disconnection from the holy ground around us, beneath us, within us. Sometime this week—take off your shoes and experience the Holy!

# ROLLER COASTER FAITH

Not long ago, someone was sharing with me a little about their journey in faith and their relationship with God. Very early on in the conversation, she likened her travels with God to those of a roller coaster ride. While I don't remember much about the specifics (my conversation partner, in fact, was rather short on the "specifics" this time around), I got stuck musing on the image of the roller coaster—and actually, how much I have always enjoyed them. Well, if truth were told, "always" is a bit of a stretch.

My history with roller coasters didn't begin with love at first sight. When I was a young boy, our family managed the luxury of a brief summer vacation at Cedar Point in Sandusky, Ohio. Due to a sudden growth spurt that summer, I was just tall enough to touch the line that allowed a rider onto the infamous "Blue Streak," a monster of a roller coaster that still scares the daylights out of a new generation of thrill seekers. My dad seemed to be pleased that I hit the mark, but as I gazed up at the towering first hill climb of the Blue Streak, I was petrified. In my nascent days of amusement park adventures, I was leery of the spinning teacups, let alone jostling my way through the hairpin turns and chiropractic thrusts of a wooden coaster.

I recall my dad working his fatherly magic to console me that I was "big" enough and "brave" enough to handle the Blue Streak (and to stop crying like a baby!), but I had serious doubts on both accounts. Once we got far enough along in the line, there was no turning back; and the worst, I now figured, was that I'd go down in a blaze ("blue," of course) of glory and my father, too—justified punishment for coaxing me onto this wood-and-steel terrorist!

Perhaps due to the Blue Streak's ability to scare away any shred of sanity that still remained in me, I eventually fell in love with roller coasters, and I have enjoyed them ever since (although, I'm not quite as fast to throw caution to the wind, or my bones into motion-trauma, as I used to be). My favorite has been the "Jack Rabbit," a 1921 masterpiece of a roller coaster in Kennywood Park, West Mifflin, PA, that plunges riders through a 40-foot natural, tree-lined ravine. The best part of the 1 minute, 15 second start-to-finish careening ride is the last "dip" that jolts you out of your seat.

Indeed, any "ride" with God is much like the roller coaster experience—just look at the travails of the Israelites after the Exodus from Egypt, or the twists and turns, bumps and grinds of the 3-year spin taken by the apostles and disciples with Jesus. There are momentous climbs up Sinai-like mountains and vertiginous drops into gardens of agony. Sometimes the events of life and the demands of staying faithful to God flash before us so quickly that we don't know what hit us. Often, before we really enter into the thrill of knowing and loving God, we must first make that long, drawn-out, clickity-clackity climb up that initial hill. There are times when the waiting (as there always is in any amusement park for the ever-popular coaster rides) to see and understand the "inscrutable ways" of God is nerve-wracking and nearly intolerable. Much like a roller coaster ride, we rarely get to see what's ahead of us or behind us—often we simply react as the twists and turns come. The undulating waves of life, much like they do in a coaster ride, set our stomachs to spinning, and we look to God to calm those dyspeptic fears.

But one thing is certain, whether we approach our journey with God with unbridled, know-no-fear enthusiasm, or whether we reluctantly inch our way along, sometimes being cajoled by someone wiser and braver than ourselves—the "ride" with God is always more than we can imagine...gets our blood pumping...and lifts us beyond the mundane track of life.

# UPON ENTERING THE EYE OF THE HURRICANE:

## *MEETING THE GOD WHO STIRS UP THE SEAS*

As I sit at the dining room table, my eyes jockeying back and forth between the window of my computer screen and the window to my front yard, both "windows," at the moment, opening unto similar worlds, the passing vestiges of Hurricane Floyd are still whipping the mighty oaks that line my street. The vibrant branches, the ones still full of the juices of life are swaying, stirred by the power of the unseen winds aloft, while the decaying branches, the ones clinging desperately to their former grandeur, are being cut loose and now litter the landscape. The gloomy, steel gray sky still casts pallor over my world this day, while the promise of rebirth and renewal waits in the wings, ready to appear upon cue.

My restlessness of spirit, which set in yesterday morning, has yet to dissipate completely. The visions of a night spent half sleeping, half waking are still alive, visions whose eerie quality surely rival any current celluloid, box office thriller promising to raise the hairs on one's neck far beyond military cadet attention. Striking scenes, captured *ad nauseum* on television news films, narrated by storm-blown reporters, reporters who continue to stand their water-logged ground while at the same time criticizing as foolish those who have stayed behind to "ride out the storm," reveal the awesome power and incredible rage of nature, and the undeniable vulnerability we all face when a mighty wind sweeps through our normal plans and programs.

As our local scene is being surveyed more closely than a deadly germ under an atomic microscope, little attention is being given to those whose vulnerability is far greater than ours, those who always live on the edge of human existence, clinging just as desperately to life as the brittle, scale-covered, life-sapped oak branches perilously perched above my house. While we are now collectively "counting our blessings," a slight nod is slowly being offered for those whom, I would presume we have to say, at least according to our strange sort of understanding of "blessing," were not "blessed" and who now set about picking up the debris of their broken lives, while the rest of us pick up the token debris of our rich and abundant lives.

From the sounds of all the reports, most people, surprisingly, faced the threat of this awesome force of nature with "respect" for its dangerous life-force. A few folks, who were gingerly bestowed the title of "brave" by newscasters, seemed determined rather to show their foolishness and disregard for powers greater than themselves, hoping to avoid being a "tragedy" in the aftermath of the hurricane. Indeed, the aura of fear seemed to touch the souls of countless people, a dis-ease settled into the fiber of everyday life, and perhaps, our vulnerability was allowed to rise to the surface, and we were permitted to touch it, to hold it, to meet it without condemnation or ridicule. In this case, somehow we felt "permission" to know our vulnerability, even in the midst of the safeties and securities that we constantly surround ourselves with.

While this reflection may seemingly be taking on the sounds of a post-hurricane Sunday morning commentary worthy of the late Charles Kuralt, it is no mere "dear diary" entry meant to capture the human side of sinking millibars and maximum sustained winds, but rather a shared reflection upon my momentary experience of fear, vulnerability, and the now more tangible description of a God whose presence has been likened to this devastating whirlwind of energetic rage. The Psalmist proclaims, as he grapples with describing the magnitude of the Creator God:

*You make the clouds your chariot; you travel on wings of the wind. You make the winds your messengers (Psalm 104).*

The Psalmist knows the sheer power and majesty of God's presence, especially through God's word/voice, as he likens it to the frightful force of a mighty storm: *The voice of the Lord is over the waters, the God of glory thunders, the Lord, over vast waters. The voice of the Lord is mighty; the voice of the Lord is majestic...The voice of the Lord twists the oaks and strips the forests (Psalm 29).*

In my restless fear and vulnerable uncertainty, the approach of Hurricane Floyd brought me face to face with this God whose voice breaks and twists and brings asunder all that we build up and construct to give ourselves false security. As these mighty winds blew and the seas raged around me, God rode them like a grand chariot. In the watching and waiting and listening, in the hoping and praying and wondering, God did indeed make these hurricane winds his messenger to me.

In the Book of the prophet Isaiah, it is the Lord God *who stirs up the sea so that its waves roar (51:15).* In a world where we send reconnaissance planes into the eye of storms and depend upon computer-generated models and infrared water vapor technologies to give us the impression of controlling the forces of nature, it seems nearly impossible to taste the true flavor of sacred scriptures, which rely upon a completely different worldview to bring life to their experiences of God. Vicariously experiencing the strength of Hurricane Floyd, watching the winds batter the coasts in its path, cringing at the mighty waves pummeling the shores that only hours before held surfers and sunbathers in their restful grasp, I was able to enter more fully into the experience of God whose qualities are compared to the forces of nature.

## UPON ENTERING THE EYE OF THE HURRICANE

Not unlike standing in the face of Hurricane Floyd, standing in the face of a God who stirs up the sea so that its waves roar reveals our absolute vulnerability, a vulnerability we work so hard to mask in our everyday comings and goings, but whose existence and ever-present disease lurks precariously near the surface of our placid lives. It is surely this recognition of vulnerability that led our forbearers in faith to declare the virtue of fear of the Lord. For the ancients, the beginning of wisdom was deeply rooted in fear of the Lord. For us "moderns" the elimination of fear seems the goal of our wisdom. Yet, throughout the movements of Christian spirituality through the ages, fear of the Lord has been more interpreted as a force meant to keep us at a "proper" distance from God rather than a force which humbly draws us into the circle of God's life. As we might say in common parlance, there is "healthy" and "unhealthy" fear of the Lord.

Over the past day or so, I have wrestled with this ancient experience of fear of the Lord, trying to make the movement from fear which intimidates, overpowers and cripples me, to an appreciation of fear that allows me to become more intimate with God, a fear that leads to deep, tangible, AWE. It is not the kind of "awe" I have experienced while watching incredible athletes flying through the air and contorting their bodies seemingly beyond human limits at the *Cirque du Soleil*, not the breathtaking vastness of a pinnacle perch high in the Sierras, nor the "awe" which comes from the tenderness of accompanying a person as they breathe their last taste of this earthly life. There are elements of these "awes" rippling through this current experience—the exhilarating rush, the heart-stopping wonder, the heart-warming peace—but this one is different.

For the first time, through this precariously frightening tremor of nature, I have come in touch with the God whose power is greater than I could ever imagine, whose being permeates all that I survey and even more, the myriad realities which exist beyond my limited capacities, someone who invites me to live in this incredible presence rather than shrink from it or be overwhelmed by it. Rather than being rendered incapable of acting, of responding to the pressures of life around me (my normal reaction to fear), this holy fear has cracked open another way of responding, another way of encountering those things which are larger than my life. It is the way of surrender.

This surrender, however, is not one in which we see ourselves, our souls evaporate like water on a scorching hot day, but rather a surrender which is a giving over of our whole selves, the persons who we are, strength and weakness, grace and sin, beauty and ugliness, hope and despair, demon and deity. Surrendering in awe to the God who stirs up the sea so that its waves roar has today brought a momentary peace which has been previously unachievable.

I am not confident that this awareness will be permanently inscribed in my soul; I am certain, like our ancient (and not-so-ancient) forbearers in faith that I will often retreat into my previous ways of dealing with fear. I will still need to hear the voices of prophets and seers; I will still need to enter deeply into rituals which have the power to transport me into a realm that is pristine and pure, free of the heavy encumbrances of my daily living; I will still need to come face to face with powers that are greater than myself when they choose to make their way onto the landscape of my life. Yet, I am thankful for this "surprise" meeting with the God-of-Surprises, this God whom I so often feel as if I know as surely as I know the wardrobe hanging in my closet or the digits of my Social Security number. I am grateful that God chooses to expose me to the kind of fear, which has the ability, when responded to with reverent surrender, to draw me into a more intimate experience of God.

As the clock's arms have journeyed since beginning this reflection, as the power which has been stirred up to fill this technological window begins to dissipate, not unlike the power sweeping the boughs I see through the window of this room, I'm left with a thankful heart for the fleeting, though impressionable glimpse of that wondrous biblical sense of awe, which, as Kathleen Norris relates in her book *Amazing Grace*, allows us to recognize the holy in our midst; as well as fear, which gives us the courage to listen and to let God awaken in us capacities and responsibilities we have been afraid to contemplate.

# THOSE LONG SUMMER NIGHTS

In the recently named Pulitzer Prize winning novel, *Gilead*, by Marilynne Robinson, the central character of the book, Reverend John Ames, is writing an extended letter to his young son of seven, about his own life and that of his forbearers. He is doing so because his present terminal heart condition, at the grand age of 76, will not afford him the opportunity to see his child grow into a man, and thus Ames will be denied the ability to share the family legacy with his son first hand.

As Reverend Ames recalls many touching and gripping events of his own boyhood, he struck a chord with me when he briefly described some long summer nights:

*"We played catch in the evenings after supper till the sun went down and it was too dark for us to see the ball."*

Indeed, I remember many a boyhood summer, with those ever-so-long-lasting hours of daylight affording us extended opportunities for baseball, as well as kickball and other childhood games. Not caring much for the science of it all, we simply assumed that those extra hours of sunlight were intended as God's gift to us children for having suffered through all those months of school. And now that we were released from the bondage of the classroom, we were free to run and play as long as we could, sort of making up for all that lost time buried in the books!

As I think back on those nights, I can picture my friends and me, much as Reverend Ames recalls, playing baseball well beyond the twilight. The fact that the ball was getting harder and harder to see with the descent of nightfall did little to drag us off the street. In fact, the team who happened to be behind in the score always wanted to keep playing, in the sure hope that with the darkness came the great opportunity for more errors—and thus more runs to score—and thus a last gasp chance for victory! When this turn of events did actually occur, of course it was the now triumphant team who declared without argument: "Let's quit now…it's way too dark! Somebody might get hurt!"

I can still hear my mother or grandmother's voice calling out to us, telling us to come inside. Enough was enough, as far as they were concerned, and running around the neighborhood or playing ball in the street after dark was flirting with disaster.

We, of course, had no concept of "enough was enough." It is inherently not in the nature of a child to grasp this very adult admonition. For us, there was never "enough" time to do the things we wanted to do, to live the life we were enjoying each day. We tried to squeeze as much out of every minute of every day that we possibly could, as much as life would allow us—even if it meant battling the dropping curtain of night on the day's larger-than-life stage of events. We were always begging for more—one more "minute" before we come in...one last television show before bedtime...one more chat on the corner with friends before taking a bath...one more fly ball in the mitt before it bopped us in the head.

As children drinking in the fullness of summer nights, we seemed to be caught up in a way of magnanimous living that would never end.

John's Gospel reminds us what the true purpose of Jesus and the Spirit's presence is in God's creation and our lives. Jesus proclaims: *"A thief comes only to steal and slaughter and destroy.* ***I came so that they might have life and have it more abundantly (John 10:10).****"*

Perhaps as adults, we may find ourselves lamenting those days when we embraced life with zest and fullness—the way Jesus apparently intended us to do so. Oh yes, indeed we still may be squeezing out every ounce of daylight we can and carrying on our activities well into the dark, but it seems now we are doing so more out of desperation and despair, ending our days incredibly tired, our energies spent, and wondering how we'll be able to get up and do it all over again tomorrow. In the glory of those long summer nights, our parents stood wide-eyed and amazed at our unending energies, as we kids wanted to embrace tomorrow as a long absent grandmother fresh back from a wonderful vacation and bearing lots of souvenir gifts for us!

On closer inspection of the Gospels, it is clear that Jesus didn't simply intend just any kind of "abundance" in life. Jesus' abundance is always a matter of *quality* over quantity. Jesus offers a particular kind of abundance, one that invigorates us rather than debilitates us, one that lifts us up rather than weighs us down, one that liberates us rather than makes us slaves to our jobs, commitments, families, and myriad responsibilities.

I wonder, in the poignant scenes we so lovingly like to recall from the scriptures, where Jesus is calling the little children, inviting them to "Come to me," whether or not these encounters happened on long summer nights. If they did, I can see Jesus inviting them to draw near…and they in turn begging for just "one more minute"…and he in turn gently smiling at their zest for abundant life—and then declaring so aptly, "To such as these little ones belongs the Kingdom of God."

# CALLING US BY NAME

Everything was going along so well. Refreshing Gulf breezes wafting over the pool area; a cloudless sky permitting the sun's full intensity to bake my skin to its proper doneness (of course, SPF applied adequately); the relaxing quiet of early morning pervading the atmosphere. Yes, everything was going so well. A few other adults beside myself sipping coffee or ice tea, already deeply immersed in their vacation-sized novels or the pages of USA Today—a perfect picture of vacation tranquility worthy of gracing the best travel brochure, truly a marketing director's dream come true.

Everything was going so well…until the kids arrived! Suddenly, the peaceful haven that had been created around the pool was disrupted. It was the beginning of the end. Jolted from my trance, I realized that another "vacation scene" was now being painted, and if the pattern held true for another day, the calm would not return until around 4 P.M., when the now tired and cranky children (and parents) would be shuffled off for an early-bird dinner or a late afternoon nap.

The first family to arrive each day during this particular week of vacation covered all the bases. Fortunately for them, their bungalow was not far from pool side, so they easily managed to bring all the "necessary" equipment required for a day spent at the pool: snacks of every variety, which rivaled even the most well-stocked convenience store; the locker-esque cooler loaded with drinks (I think it took the whole day for the hotel's ice machine to replenish itself after they got into it!); inflatable toys of every imaginable shape, size and color, representing at least one half of the animals Noah took into the ark; goggles, flippers, snorkels, sun lotions, CD players. I couldn't help but wonder if they had driven from Wisconsin in a Greyhound bus in order to accommodate everything that was needed to make this vacation successful!

Everything had been going so well…and then the silence was broken. As the remaining families continued to filter in for their day at the pool (I kept wanting to tell them: Hey folks, there's a big, beautiful beach and LOTS of water over there—leave this area for old folks and vacationing priests!), I eventually took notice of some of the dynamics between parents and children.

As the morning went by, I became particularly attuned to a young mother who was keeping a watchful eye on her son and daughter as they played in and around the water. (I specifically say "eye," because the other eye she tried to give some rest as she stretched out on a lounge chair, hoping to catch a few moments of relaxation for herself). I was very much aware of her attentiveness, which is not surprising given the ages of her children and the number of other kids in the pool (many of whom did not seem to be blessed with "attentive" parents). Even more so, I gradually became fascinated by the number of times she called their names!

At first, it struck me as annoying. I must have heard "Anthony" and "Katarina," or the more familiar, "Kat" countless times in the space of the first 5 minutes after their arrival! At first, it was almost as annoying to me as listening to the seemingly endless chatter of children calling out "Marco Polo" as they bobbed in and out of the water. I quickly tried to distract myself by thinking about getting a dollar for every time I heard one of their names! Unfortunately, it didn't work; even with the thought of raking in millions, I couldn't keep up!

"Anthony, leave your sister alone!"

"Anthony, use your own goggles!"

"Katarina, leave your brother and his goggles alone; you have your own!"

"Anthony, don't take the Doritos into the pool."

"Katarina, stay off the ledge, you're going to fall."

"Katarina, leave that boy alone; he doesn't want to kiss your Mickey Mouse floaties!"

"Anthony, you just had a snack."

"Katarina, quit whining; Anthony, quit making your sister whine!"

"Anthony...Katarina...."

It was a constant flow—addressing them about every move they made, or for that matter, every move they didn't make. At some point, I discovered that I had passed beyond the "annoyed" state and into a more "reflective" state. Perhaps the constant recitation of the children's names worked like a soothing mantra, the repetition of which helped me enter a more elevated plain of thought.

As parents always appear to be, and rightly so, Anthony and Katarina's mother was consumed with letting them know she was there—calling them by name, not only to get their attention, but mostly to reassure them of her abiding (although, not totally undivided) attention.

I was struck, at first, by the sheer multiplication of their names—wondering why more parents don't suffer from laryngitis! Of course, recalling my own youth, I also wondered at what point kids become immune or deaf to hearing their names being called.

BUT THEN…it dawned on me—how fortunate they are to have a mother looking after them with such nurturing care and vigilance. And I wondered, in a flight of fancy, if this is how the loving parent God acts with me, with us? Is God constantly calling my name with the same vigilance?

Almost immediately, I started humming the tune and hearing the words to one of my favorite hymns, *You Are Mine* by David Haas (#649 in the Gather hymnal):

## CALLING US BY NAME

*I will come to you in silence; I will lift you from all your fear.*
*You will hear my voice, I claim you as my choice,*
*Be still and know I am here.*
*Do not be afraid, I am with you. I have called you each by name.*
*Come and follow me, I will bring you home;*
*I love you and you are mine.*

And I wonder…does God get laryngitis? Does God tire of saying my name? Is God watching out for me and calling for my attention when I start to venture where I don't belong (or when I'm already there!)? At what point do I become immune or deaf to God's voice calling my name? I wonder if God, like a parent, uses different names for different situations, depending upon the importance of the matter, or the level of my attentiveness: Ben…Benjamin Albert…Benny…Benji (Yikes! I hope not; I gave that nickname up long ago in grade school!)….Fr. Berinti!

There are many places to turn in the scriptures when we raise questions about God calling our names. And although we often become like young children; unable to hear and receive God's attentiveness to us; distracted by our own desires and entertainment, buried under our own brooding concerns and tribulations; misled by others calling our names with more vigor; presenting more intoxicating offers than we believe God is offering—God continues to call; God knows us each by name; God seeks us out when we are lost.

In the course of any given week, I sometimes feel

the same way that I imagine Anthony and Katarina felt that lazy summer day in June—annoyed by their mother's voice calling them by name. Sometimes, I am so distracted by others calling my name, looking for me to respond to their desires, and requests, and suggestions, that I fail to hear, fail to discern the voice of God calling me.

Sometimes, I wonder if God is calling my name…and sometimes I wonder how often I miss hearing God calling my name. If you find yourself asking the same questions, wondering the same things…turn to one or several of these scripture passages and be reminded of the sound of the voice we'll never want to forget!

*There an angel of the Lord appeared to him in fire flaming out of a bush…When the Lord saw him coming over to look at it more closely, God called out to him from the bush, 'Moses! Moses!' He answered, 'Here I am…' (Exodus 3:2-4)*

*The lamp of God was not yet extinguished, and Samuel was sleeping in the temple of the Lord where the ark of God was. The Lord called out to Samuel, who answered, 'Here I am,' (I Samuel 3:3-4)*

*He tells the numbers of the stars; he calls each by name. (Psalm 147:4)*

*Lift up your eyes on high and see who has created these: He leads out their army and numbers them, calling them all by name. By his great might and the strength of his power not one of them is missing. (Isaiah 40:26)*

*But now, thus says the Lord, who created you, O Jacob, and formed you, O Israel; Fear not, for I have redeemed you; I have called you by name; you are mine. (Isaiah 43:1)*

*For the sake of Jacob, my servant, of Israel my chosen one, I have called you by your name, giving you a title, though you knew me not. (Isaiah 45:4)*

*But whoever enters the gate is the shepherd of the sheep. The gatekeeper opens it for him, and the sheep hear his voice, as he calls his own sheep by name and leads them out. (John 10:2-3)*

# MUSINGS ON A 43rd BIRTHDAY: *UP, UP, AND AWAY!*

Recently, I finished reading a challenging, insightful and engaging book by Joan Anderson, *A Year by the Sea* (NY: Broadway Books, 1999). As the author recounts her "sabbatical year," removed from her marriage and her "normal" life in a quest to rediscover her true self, she shares the following: *I can barely recall when last I relinquished control to another—took a dare, really, and went off to a place I didn't know, trusting a stranger to take me there (23).*

For most of us, "relinquishing control' is a frightening prospect; most likely, no less frightening than when we first entered this world on our birth day. Yet, when we muster the courage, and perhaps the foolishness to do so, we often open ourselves to the deeper mysteries—of our true self, the relationships we cherish, and the world in which we live.

Unable to climb back into a womb and once again relive the experience of relinquishing control at the moment of birth (although, I'm sure had I searched hard enough, I could have found some "New Age" Spa in California that attempts to recreate such experiences--for a hefty price!), I yearned for some other experience that might allow me to have, as Anderson described, that sense of daring, of going off to a place I didn't know, of trusting a stranger to take me there. **So...I PARASAILED on my birthday!**

For many years, on every occasion I spent time at a beach, I would watch those brave souls being lifted into the air, sailing above the beautiful beaches and waters—and I envied them! Not really being the adventurous type, at least not when it comes to placing myself in physical danger, I found myself acting like a timid 6th grader at his very first school dance—wanting desperately to ask a girl to step onto the dance floor, and at the same time, petrified at the very thought of actually dancing in public! Even after watching the usual television news magazine reports about the victims of parasailing accidents—I still had a burning desire to go airborne.

Finally, about 7 years ago, I did the deed. I hadn't actually intended to do so, but I ended up being swept away in the excitement of the moment (and perhaps a little too much sea salt up my nostrils). I was traveling with a friend in Ft. Myers, and he decided to parasail. I joined him in the boat, and when the driver asked "how many are going up," I blurted out: BOTH of us!" It was too late...I was committed. Of course, my friend Dave was launched first—just in case there were a problem—then I'd more easily be able to back out of my end of the deal! It was a tremendous experience.

Now, seven years later, inspired by the words of Joan Anderson, my mind returned immediately to the experience of parasailing, because it seemed to contain within it the powerful challenges of which she spoke—especially the part about "trusting a stranger to take you there."

As our little parasailing crew awaited the refueling and preparation of the boat to set sail for the Gulf, we were instructed to sign and initial some papers. I didn't really bother to look at what I was signing, although I assumed it was some kind of waiver. One of the women who joined us, however, took a little more time than I did before penning her name in the appropriate blanks. With a twisted look on her face, and her budding tan beginning to drain from her skin, she declared: "Hey...it says here this can cause 'serious injury'...or even DEATH!" I'm not so sure why she was surprised to discover this possibility—after all, we'd be floating above the waters at about 900 feet, being towed by a speed boat! I suppose it was the fact that she actually saw it in print, somehow intensifying the "possibility." Another companion and I simply said, "Just sign...you're not actually supposed to READ that stuff."

Excited as I was, I did, however, pause a moment to think about what I was about to do. Indeed, I was literally "signing my life away," and would soon entrust my life and limbs to two complete strangers—a swarthy, beach combing couple who make a living putting people in danger! When I think about it, it is strange: a boat pulls into the wharf...two strangers who look to have been at sea far too long say "get in, sign here"...and moments later, you are allowing them to put you in a harness, attach you to a giant nylon mushroom contraption...and then speed away with you in tow on the end of 1200 feet of rope! I suppose my original thought, and statement to our sailing partner, was accurate—don't think about it—and certainly—don't *say* it!

Yet, the initial exhilaration of the experience began precisely with the realization that I was entrusting my whole self to someone whom I knew nothing about, but whom I believed was about to take me on an adventure, take me to a place where I might see a new perspective, enjoy a freedom from the constraints of my daily drudgery. Somehow, to truly be liberated, it seems that a "stranger" might have to play some part in that liberation.

I think of the "liberation" Matthew the tax collector experienced when the *stranger*, Jesus of Nazareth came and ate with him amidst the bevy of "sinners" who gathered under his roof. How about how the Woman at the Well became so free that she began a new way of living and proclaiming God—but only after entrusting the intimacies of her private life to a "stranger," someone who should have been following the law of his religious tradition and kept his distance from her. Then there's the infamous encounter between the strangers on the road to Jericho, where one man, barely recognizable because of the beating he had received at the hands of robbers, is tended to by another man with more compassion and generosity than could be found in the hearts and actions of two religious leaders, who simply passed by without so much as a whimper. Yes, it seems that there are occasions when we taste of freedom only after it has been offered by a stranger, rather than by those with whom we are most familiar.

As I was launched from the platform of the boat, I felt the overwhelming sense of JOY! Always one to rush ahead instead of trying to "stay in the moment," I was determined not to concentrate on the sad fact that in fifteen minutes I'd be back to earth, but rather to allow those fifteen minutes of bliss to seem eternal. It seemed that my whole body was smiling! As I drifted higher and higher, the swimmers in the water and the bathers on the beach turned to cinder specks, the roar of the speeding boat's engine faded away, and an incredible QUIET and STILLNESS overcame me.

In a simple, but beautiful poem by O.B. Hardison, Jr., I find the words to describe the scene:

*The sky unfolds into the water.*
*Clouds blossom in the water and the shore flames*
*with the glory of their opening*
*As though God were making the world again.*

Amidst the quiet and stillness, floating at what seemed to be the slow-motion pace of time-elapsed photography, a freshness, a renewal, a re-making seemed to be in progress, and I simply drew in every breath as if it were both my first...and my last. Perhaps more than any other feeling or sensitivity throughout the adventure, it was the quiet and stillness that was most pervasive. Rising high above the din and clatter of life, the tranquility was mesmerizing, intoxicating. Not that I needed any more convincing, since I am a firm believer, practitioner, and promoter of the absolute necessity for people to carve out regular, defined niches for quiet and solitude, I reaffirmed my beliefs beyond any shadow of doubt. As I drifted into a kind of an alert oblivion, I realized that I didn't need to take to these heights in order experience the peace and tranquility that was mine, since I was equally aware that this sensation has come to me while walking quietly along the beach, kneeling before the Blessed Sacrament in our church, strolling the wooden deck of the "Closer Walk" at the San Pedro Spiritual Center, or even while dining alone in a restaurant, absorbed in a good book.

In the midst of the quiet and stillness, I suddenly realized—I'm NOT STILL! I am moving—and moving at a pretty hefty pace! In that moment, these two seemingly opposite experiences became one, and the cherished words of my favorite poet, T.S. Eliot, literally came to life. I've always understood the meaning and sentiment behind them, but now I was actually living them in a tangible, incredibly physical way.

In the series of poems, *The Four Quartets*, Eliot explores

an ancient spiritual truth and icon—the *still point.* In the first of the quartets, *Burnt Norton*, Eliot entertains the nature of the *still point*:

*At the still point of the turning world. Neither*
*flesh nor fleshless;*
*Neither from nor towards; at the still point,*
*there the dance is,*
*But neither arrest nor movement. And do*
*not call it fixity,*
*Where past and future are gathered. Neither*
*movement from nor towards,*
*Neither ascent nor decline. Except for the point*
*the still point,*
*There would be no dance, and there is only*
*the dance.*

Later in the poem, *East Coker*, Eliot concludes:

*Love is most nearly itself*
*When here and now cease to matter.*
*We must be still and still moving*
*Into another intensity*
*For a further union, a deeper communion....*

High above Bradenton and Holmes Beaches, I was overcome with the sensation of "being still...and still moving." This physical experience is what lies at the heart of the whole spiritual life. Throughout the length and breadth of the Christian experience, spiritual writers have long plumbed the depth of what it means to be centered in God...and at the same time, be moving with God. The dangers of the spiritual life for all Christians swim at the far ends of the spectrum: either over-activity in the name of God and the Gospel of Jesus Christ, or under-activity, which cultivates the misguided sense that we do nothing while God pulls the strings. Either perspective is twisted and misses the recurring truth scattered throughout the scriptures and the history of spiritual practice.

We would find it increasingly difficult to move into any kind of deeper union, deeper communion with God and creation without cultivating the practice of quiet, solitude, release from activity and movement. Yet, the truth about God is that in the midst of the stillness, God can and does move us. To be in contemplation is hardly an action that is dominated and directed by our work and desires, but rather by God's words and deeds. This spiritual truth, this spiritual discipline has become an even more tremendous challenge in a culture such as ours, which glorifies constant (even if often pointless) *activity*—DOING superseding BEING. Many people know no "still point" within their "universe," and clearly suffer for it.

Joan Anderson relinquished control of her life by disconnecting from all the demands and expectations, all the accretions of "supposed tos" that had melded themselves to her life like barnacles on an oversized, drifting seashell.

She went to a "place," more spiritual than physical, she didn't know, in order to know more.

Every day, we venture on our pilgrim way toward God, filling our lives with countless expectations and demands, familiar attitudes and behaviors, rarely having the courage to relinquish anything, let alone the intimate depths of our souls—although lumpy, scratchy and harsh, I suppose we become accustomed to our "barnacles." Yet, the still point to whom we journey, the One who knows no past, present or future, but knows only eternity, invites us to let go, to soar beyond, to rise above our familiar terrain, and on occasion, to take a dare, to really place ourselves in the hands of a "stranger," and to be led to a *greater intensity, a deeper union, a deeper communion.*

# AUTUMN

*"This I try to remember when time's measure*
*painfully chafes, for instance when autumn*
*flares out at the last, boisterous and like us longing*
*to stay—how everything lives, shifting*
*from one bright vision to another, forever*
*in these momentary pastures."*

*Mary Oliver (American Primitive)*

*Along the spiritual journey of life, we often long to stay, linger, and even make a home in one particular place or another, and yet, autumn always invites us in another direction. We are always shifting, with restless hearts, from life to death and death to life. As the leaves fall and the weather turns to a dampening chill, let us try to remember, we are a pilgrim people, always "on the way."*

# HAVING TO LET GO:
## *THE BUS IS HERE!*

I made a slower than normal drive down the street on my way to work today. I did this for two reasons—actually one reason, two pieces. Today is the first day of school.

As the children and young people start making their way to the bus stops on the first few days of school, and the bright yellow "think tanks" begin clogging the local arteries, all of us need to slow down and pay more attention.

Today is the first day of school, so I am driving more slowly this morning, not only to safeguard the kids, but more importantly, to drink in the thrill of this day. As I inch down the street, I spy several clusters of elementary school children along the way. I can't quite figure out, given the weight and exercise problems that have infiltrated the lives of our youth, why the bus stops are so plentiful within such a short distance. I chuckle to see the same mom, whom I've watched for the past two years, again *drive* her little one exactly three houses down from theirs to the bus stop!

I marvel at the variety of emotion painted on the faces of the kids—some clearly petrified; some as nonchalant as a ticket taker at the movies; some as jumpy as a Cirque du Soleil acrobat; some walking more slowly than grandpa on his walker, hoping the bus will come and go so they can return home to squeeze out a little more summertime leisure.

But really it's the faces of the parents who accompany their kids, and watching their weak attempts to remain stoic while clearly on the verge of a breakdown, that warm my heart. Grace made it possible that I was stopped for several minutes by the bus cross-arm, and I was able to relish the scene of one, newly minted first-grader mounting the bus steps. Dad had the video camera going (dads always seem to occupy themselves with tasks and gadgets during emotional moments, that way they can "appear" strong and in control); mom was decked out in sunglasses, partly because the morning blaze was already beating down from the sky, but mostly, I think, to hide her tears, not wanting to traumatize her little girl more than she already was on the first day of school. As the doors closed, and dad continued his filming, mom waved goodbye, and brushed the tears from her check, just beneath the cover of those brilliant blue Oakleys. With the smoked windows of the bus, I'm sure the little girl never saw those tears (nor did mom see hers).

As the proud parents joined hands and began the slow

trek home, I couldn't help but think today is just one of many more occasions to come when they will be called upon to LET GO. Some will be worthy of preserving on film, while others will be too painful to even want to recall. Some will be planned and necessary, while others will take them by frightening surprise. Some occasions of letting go will feel good, and their confidence in a job well done will swell, while others will leave them wringing their hands and asking the unanswerable question, "how did we get to this?"

While I have never walked a child to their first day of school and had to bid them a tearful goodbye, I was moved by this morning's scene because we all are called upon to LET GO—and I've done plenty of it in my own lifetime. This morning's picture will remain with me, I think, as a metaphor for what letting go means, asks, and requires of each of us— whether or not we are willing participants.

When we find ourselves asked to let go of someone or something dear to us, it helps to have someone along for the walk. Our companion may not be able to change our situation, they may not be able to substitute for what or who we had to release, they may not fully understand our grief over this loss—but having someone to keep pace with us, to see us along the way is a gift—and we can be that same gift to someone else who is struggling with letting go.

When we find ourselves asked to let go of someone or

something that holds deep meaning in our lives, it helps to be reminded that the followers of Jesus, and the Lord himself, were no strangers to this challenging sorrow. John's gospel provides wonderful vignettes contained in Jesus' "farewell discourses" that help us to see the emotion-laden heart of the Lord as he began to break away from his beloved disciples. And in these vignettes, perhaps we can find strength and comfort for our own letting go.

We also witness the struggle of the disciples, as they try to cope, in wide-eyed disbelief, with their Master's departure. They were to shed more than a few tears between the cross and resurrection, and the pain of his departure testified to the depth of love they possessed for Jesus.

And isn't that the kick in the stomach for us all—the deeper the love, the more painful the separation; the more profound the connection, the harder to let go. Sometimes, after having limped away from too many painful partings at the "bus stops" of our lives, we may choose to limit our connections with people or commitments; we may choose to spare ourselves the pain of parting by never entering a deep relationship in the first place. Letting go is painful, and so we find our defenses—and sometimes, we never again emerge from those protective shells.

If all of our life's separating were as touching as saying goodbye on that first day of school, we wouldn't mind the tears, and we'd be thrilled to pull out the video in the years to come. But most of our letting go takes us far beyond sentimental bus stops and airport farewells. Most of our letting go leaves scars on the heart, scars so painful that we perhaps wish we didn't have a heart that could so easily be bruised and broken.

In the original text of Frank Baum's *The Wonderful Wizard of Oz*, the Tin Woodman returns to the Wizard, anxiously seeking his heart. But the Wizard warns him: "I think you are wrong to want a heart. It makes most people unhappy. If you only knew it, you are in luck not to have a heart."

To which, the Tin Woodman replies: "That must be a matter of opinion; for my part, I will bear all the unhappiness without a murmur, if you will give me the heart."

Indeed, having a heart means that we will bear the pain of unhappiness, and much more. Our occasions for letting go will test the capacity of our hearts to love, to forgive, to honor, and to fill with compassion.

Sooner or later, the bus will be here again...and we'll be saying goodbye. But the deep and meaningful bonds that we forge with people and the most important commitments we make need not unravel completely with every goodbye. Sometimes letting go only allows for a richer and more grace-filled *coming back*!

# HUNGER IN THE LAND OF PLENTY: *AN EPISODE OF BACK TO SCHOOL SHOPPING*

I should have known better than to head to the mall for a few quick stops the other night! After all, my destination was serving up a dangerous cocktail of back to school shoppers and tax-free power buying! Needless to say, the place was swamped, and my visit was anything but quick. As I stepped into the main fairway of the mall, I almost pulled my too-many-people-waiting-for-a-table maneuver—a speedy about face when I anticipate that my "table for two" dinner will actually be served by tomorrow morning's breakfast! But, I was determined not to back down in fear from the hordes of children and grumpy teens that were covering every square inch of space like ants at a gourmet picnic spread—and so I forged ahead.

While walking past a store whose window mannequins seemed draped in rags similar to those I just dusted my furniture with earlier in the day, I caught sight and sound of a mother and teenage daughter in stage three of a violent argument. Obviously, even to the untrained eye and ear, these two had been going at it full tilt, were completely exasperated, and clearly ready to toss one or the other over the edge of the escalator steps. Of course, it was all over the impossible task of finding adequately styled clothes for the beginning of school.

While I personally have not had the displeasure of engaging in this annual rite of passage, I have been privy to lots of tears and fears about it. Even in schools with strict uniform codes, back to school wardrobe purchases can still create significant angst, as there never seem to be enough properly striped (or non-striped) sneakers to go around Central Florida.

What tugged at my heart, as I faintly listened to the argument and watched the blood pressures rising, was this exchange of words:

**Mom:** "I cannot believe…in this entire mall…you haven't been able to find at least ONE outfit to wear for next week! We've looked everywhere—now what are we going to do?"

**Daughter: "**You are so mean! I can't help it—***there's nothing here!*"**

And that was the clincher! "There's nothing here!" In one building, with more merchandise than a person can find in an entire third world country, this shopper's lament was: "there's nothing here!"

But let's not jump only on the teenager's case—all of us have probably uttered these same words while bubbling over in despair, standing in the midst of an absurd amount of plenty!

Throughout the Gospels, Jesus, like the prophets of old, particularly Isaiah, sets out to smash to pieces the LIE OF SCARCITY. From not enough love to go around to enemies, to not enough compassion for the disinherited, to merely "five loaves and two fish" to feed multitudes of mouths after a long day of preaching and teaching—Jesus confronts our misguided notion of what is enough.

How often do we come up against the LIE OF SCARCITY in our own lives? Not enough firepower to squelch terrorists. Not enough food to feed the poor in Africa—after all, they just misuse our help anyway. Not enough money for equal educational opportunities in our communities. Not enough vibrant and engaged parishioners to ignite a tempest under the pews of our parish. Not enough patience to create a balanced household. Not enough of the "right" people to settle down with in a loving, life-giving marital relationship. Not enough caring teachers to guide me toward my goals in life. Not enough bandages to heal my broken heart. Not enough "I'm sorry" to make me let go of the hurt. Not enough....

Sometimes, it is the very overwhelming wealth that surrounds us that blinds us to the truth on the other side of the lie of scarcity. We become so nonplussed by the enormous amount of products and choices and options set before us that we are paralyzed. And in our paralysis, we have nothing else to say but... "there's nothing here!"

In the various renditions of the "loaves and the fish" accounts in the Gospels, there is never any mention that somehow, the loaves and fish (which are accounted in various amounts, depending upon the evangelist) are miraculously replicated or multiplied. All that is said is that when these gifts are turned over to the Lord, and people are called to take responsibility for whatever it is that they have and possess, there will always be more than enough—fragments a plenty left over for those who will continue to be in need after the feasting takes place. While Jesus' apostles want to fan the flames of the lie of scarcity—"all we have are a few loaves and couple of fish"—Jesus douses that misguided fire and invites them to partake in the only "miracle" available—people serving one another in communion with God.

Hanging our heads in guilt over our greed and the silliness of saying, "there's nothing here," will not advance the Gospel and the Reigning of God. As the followers of Christ, we are invited to share our gifts—in whatever amount they may be. To turn them over to the Lord, who clearly has banished the word "scarcity" from God's vocabulary, and who must smile on our foolish, greedy self-indulgences, while at the same time nudging us to push past these sins.

Hunger in the land of plenty? Is the problem a lack of goods—or is the problem a lack of distribution? When

Jesus fed the multitudes, the miracle they experienced was one of communion—a communion of wealth where everyone responded to the invitation: "***You*** give them something to eat!"

# THE EARTHINESS OF GOD

There has always been a *tension* in living the Christian faith between immersing ourselves in this world and running away from it. At any given time in our Church's history, these two approaches have vied for acceptance. Quite often, however, the urge to run away from the world, to condemn the world, or to weep and grind our teeth in this "vale of tears" has taken precedence over getting into the thick of our world and finding the wonder and beauty amidst the suffering and struggle. There is plenty of spiritual vocabulary, plenty of saintly writings, and plenty of preachers that would have us fold up our tents and run for the hills. When anyone of us takes a serious look at the world in which we live, the temptation is hard to avoid. But avoid it we must! You see, our Catholic faith has a sticky belief that is hard to hide—it's called the

INCARNATION. Remember that fancy word... it's what we commemorate in a special way at Christmas. The Incarnation is our belief that God becomes flesh in Jesus of Nazareth. It is in and through the person of Jesus that we are invited to a deeper relationship with God,

The beauty of our Catholic faith Tradition is that we *root* our experience of God IN DAILY HUMAN EXPERIENCE. We bring *our bodies and souls*, our entire selves, to the living of our faith. As a people called and gifted by God through our Baptism, you and I do not follow some nebulous "philosophy" of life; we don't place our life's hopes and dreams in the egg basket of a "moral code"; we don't nostalgically look back at some "really nice man" who lived a long time ago and who did such "nice" things for people and see in him a model for our life. Rather, we believe that God immersed God-self in this world and continues to live in it through the Body of Christ—that's you and me. There is a fundamental **earthiness** about our faith.

So often we look around us and we think that allowing my "life" to touch my "faith" (as if they are really two different things) may result in getting my faith "dirty!" We want to have a faith that is safe and clean—one that could pass the most stringent anti-bacterial test available. Yet, we need to be reminded how we were created by God in the first place—out of the elements of the earth. God, in a sense, got down and dirty, and God formed us from the earth. God wasn't afraid to touch this world, to mold it, to fashion it, to shape it into a new creation— why should we be afraid?

But what about getting away from it all? After all, isn't God fundamentally *beyond* us, isn't that what we call "transcendence"? Isn't that what we believe in saying that God is God, so far above and beyond our human ways? Doesn't a part of us want God to stay in heaven, at least so we can have some place to go to when this troubled world collapses?

Of course…these are legitimate feelings and experiences. These are very human tensions we encounter. You and I do experience a hunger and thirst for "transcendence," for "rising above and beyond" where we are in our lives at any given moment. Human experience isn't enough by itself—we desire something to be "added" to it. That "something" we desire is INTIMACY WITH GOD. We want to be able to see and touch a piece of what we believe to be above and beyond us. The problem rests not so much in the reaching out of God, who also happens to be reaching out toward us, but in those moments when we find human life to be an *obstacle* to intimacy with God and when we try to do away with our human condition, our human reality.

We cannot escape the central component of our faith—the Word became Flesh and dwelt among us—and because of this, our world has never been the same! We cannot escape the world, no matter how hard we try. As Catholics, we are called to immerse ourselves in the world, to immerse ourselves in LIFE!

During the month of October, amongst the numerous commemorations and recognitions we celebrate as a Church, we celebrate our RESPECT FOR LIFE. Many people try to reduce that call for respect to one or another "special issue." Yet, how can we be a people who respect, celebrate, honor, and cherish life, if we find ourselves running away from the life we have been given, when we find ourselves so often condemning the world and God's creatures?

Many religious traditions, including some of our fellow Christians, have a real fear of rooting our experience of God in the human. We think we know the human condition too well, and it's not the place where we want God to make a home. Yet, while we honestly try to face our real fears and doubts, our faith must continue to embrace the great truth that God became Flesh and dwells among us. This is why we RESPECT LIFE in all of its stages and variations.

# YET ANOTHER YEAR WITHOUT THE "GREAT PUMPKIN"!

Another Halloween has come and gone…and still no "Great Pumpkin" has risen out of the pumpkin patch—at least not that I'm aware of!

Funny how this holiday, once mostly the cherished domain of children and their desire to "become someone else," even just for a night, has now become yet another venue for filling commercial coffers. Halloween, another triumph of market ingenuity, is so big that a friend recently told me that a co-worker unabashedly declared that "Halloween is my *favorite* holiday!" Yikes! That's a far cry from grabbing a few candy bars with a sheet over your head and calling it a night!

While my candy scrounging and costume wearing days are well behind me, in early October, I become especially vigilant about keeping my eyes open for the annual airing of the *Peanuts* classic, *It's the Great Pumpkin, Charlie Brown* (and I'll do the same for *A Charlie Brown Christmas*). This year was a bonanza!

In the same week, PBS aired a wonderful, but sobering documentary about the life of Charles Schulz, the creator and sole illustrator of the *Peanuts* cartoon strip, and then Linus' umpteenth sojourn to the pumpkin patch followed days later. After learning more about the life of the talented, but lonely Schulz, and watching the tale of the "Great Pumpkin," it became apparent to me that both Schulz's life, and the way it was so dramatically portrayed through his signature comic strip, are testimonies to the struggle between hope and resignation, between knowing we are loved and desperately hoping we will be loved.

Even though the ending of the "Great Pumpkin" is forever the same (thank goodness there's been no sequel), and we are both bemused by Linus' ill-fated devotion as well as sympathetic to his dashed dreams, it's the unrefined ***struggle*** that keeps us coming back for a viewing. After all, what has made *Peanuts* so wildly popular for well over 50 years is that the scars and blemishes that each of us are tarnished by (and those scars and blemishes we mete out, as well) are never hidden or glossed over with a chocolate coating. Perhaps the fact that the *Peanuts* characters are children, and the television cartoon figures are voiced by children (Charles Schulz defiantly insisted to CBS that this be so—or else no show!) both make the very *adult* struggles the characters engage more palatable. We allow ourselves to see ourselves as we are, rather than to be repulsed and frightened by our human cruelty and indifference.

## YET ANOTHER YEAR WITHOUT THE "GREAT PUMPKIN"!

Linus is a testimony to the heart of the Christian message, in so far as he represents all of us who continue to dream, to believe, to hope, to await and prepare for, and to see what others fail to see behind the veil of our senses.

Somehow, despite all our "wanting-it-now-if-not-yesterday" attitudes, we can still watch the end of *It's the Great Pumpkin, Charlie Brown*, and smile warmly—knowing that so much of our life, so many of the struggles we face are more about our ability to hope and trust than about our capacity to solve and settle things.

Yes, yet another year…and no "Great Pumpkin," Linus and Charlie Brown—but you're in good company, as we, the People of God, continue to cling to the hope of a "new heavens and new earth"—despite all indications that our hope is sorely misguided.

# WHIPPING UP SOMETHING SPECIAL IN THE "LORD'S KITCHEN"

Despite the fact that dining out for the holidays is becoming increasingly more popular, most families will still spend a great deal of time in the kitchen of their own homes. There is simply nothing like a holiday kitchen brimming with the sounds and aromas of festivity. The atmosphere is electric; the bonds between family members are as sweetly knit together as the ingredients of a favorite recipe passed down from generation to generation. In this place, the hungers and thirsts of daily living are nourished far beyond what mere physical sustenance can provide.

As the Feast of Thanksgiving approaches, I am reminded that the holiday kitchen is a place like no other in a home, particularly when that same kitchen may lay relatively dormant throughout most of the year. With our hectic schedules and odd-hour meal times (if we take time to eat at all), often the only sounds coming from the kitchen are those of the beeping microwave, indicating that another "Lean Cuisine" has served its time in the "nuclear oven" and is now ready for quick consumption. I am convinced that a generation or two of young Americans today have never witnessed pots and pans on the stove nor something other than a frozen pizza baking in the oven. For them, cardboard convenience wins out over crusty casseroles any day!

At times, the modern kitchen resembles the "sacred space" of the formal living room of my youth. Remember, it was the place no one was ever allowed to enter, except on holidays and special occasions. Here was this beautiful room, outfitted with the finest furniture in the whole house, sometimes smartly covered with plastic, yet it was off limits 360+ days each year. I was never quite sure if it was the furniture that needed protecting or the array of "you-break-it-you-bought-it" collectibles that were on display. Well before reaching the age of reason, I often wondered whether or not the living room ever got lonely! It always seemed such a waste…but of course, while my sentiments may clearly have leaned toward keeping our living room company on a more regular basis, I was intelligent enough to know that entering this sanctum outside the high holy days would only lead to an "unholy" reprimand!

Kitchens are meant to be lived in, wrestled with, sullied and beaten down by overuse. All those museum-piece kitchens I salivate over in the cooking and home decor digests, beautiful as they are, don't quite match up to the character and vitality of the truly lived in, cooked in kitchen of family and friends. Jo Ann Passariello Deck, in her book *Where the Heart Is*, captures the essence of a kitchen when she reminisces about her own upbringing:

*My Italian relatives...always wanted to sit in the kitchen. They even built houses without dining rooms. Big kitchens were all they wanted. They lived their whole lives in those kitchens, around the stove eating, talking, playing cards, reading newspapers, drinking coffee. When they weren't around the stove, they were in church, in God's home....*

The kitchen was so critical to the Italian home that many people had an "extra" one built in the basement of their homes! Why two? Actually, it was put in the basement for quite practical reasons: 1) when one was into heavy "sauce" production (some call it "gravy"), there was less to damage by the splashes and splatter in thc basement kitchen; and 2) the basement, enjoying much cooler temperatures, was the perfect place to cook during the heat of the summer months! Of course, Italians are neither the first nor the last to have created a truly "sacred" space in their kitchens.

What is it about a kitchen that has the ability, when brought to life in the way just described, to become a holy place, where souls are nourished just as much, if not more so, than bodies? Bettina Vitell, in her book *A Taste of Heaven and Earth*, presents a dazzling insight:

*The kitchen is a place that sharpens us. It's a place that wakes us up. Our sense of smell becomes keener. We taste with greater subtlety. We see with more clarity and our movements become quick and sure.... Cooking requires that we be fully present. This is one of its greatest teachings.*

Perhaps it is a stretch of the imagination (and heavens knows, we often need more flexibility in our imaginations!), but as I read these potent words of Vitell, I immediately think to substitute the word "kitchen" with "church," or, even more specifically, "Mass." Try it yourself.... Seen in this light, is it any wonder that Jesus chose a fellowship meal to be the pivotal point of access into his suffering, death and resurrection for his disciples? Is it any wonder that Jesus' table fellowship, in a sense, his "hanging around kitchens" (remember, people of Jesus' time did not have the "luxury" of separate "dining areas"), resulted in numerous miracles? Is it any wonder, given the centrality and ritual holiness of preparing and sharing meals within the Jewish faith tradition, that Jesus' "kitchen fellowship" also provided the source of much of the opposition to his mission and ministry? People get close, share intimacies around the stove and table—and for Jesus' opponents, this was precisely the problem—he was too close to the wrong people! The anger and vehement opposition roused by Jesus' turning over the tables of the temple moneychangers or his alleged blasphemies against the name of God, in reality, pale in comparison to the ire he raised by being drawn into the intimacy of "kitchen fellowship" with the poor, the outcast, the lepers, and those emphatically judged unworthy of human contact, especially contact with a holy prophet! People get dirty in the kitchen…and the religious authorities of Jesus' day worked hard to stay clean!

As Christians gather around the table of the Lord, we often concentrate upon the finished product. We speak about the Mass as a "banquet table," a "meal," a time of "eating and drinking," for nourishment of body and soul. But what if we imagine the Mass not as a finished product, the end result, but as the very place of preparation, the place where we get ready to share in the meal. What if we began to see the Mass not so much as our gathering around the table, where we anticipate being waited upon and fed, but rather as the "kitchen" where we engage in the preparations of the meal, where we share the fellowship that comes from mixing and stirring, from cutting and chopping, where the liveliness of conversation reaches a fever pitch because people are truly drawing closer to one another, where the "making" is far more important, far more sustaining than is the "consuming"?

To borrow the words of Vitell, are we not drawn to worship and fellowship on the Lord's Day precisely because we desire to be "sharpened"? Are we not desirous that our senses be stimulated, our mind and heart be awakened to the presence of God in our lives, in our world? In the "kitchen of Lord," are we not in search of clearer vision, of tears gently to be wiped away, of eyes to be strengthened so as to see the path God has for each of us? Is not the Lord's kitchen the place where we prepare what we need to fortify our movements, to build up our faltering limbs, to release us from the shackles of fear, disappointment, and despair that so easily impair our freedom to follow the Lord?

If in fact we come to the Lord's kitchen seeking these gifts, searching for these insights, desiring these nourishments, then we must be attentive, engaged, and, in Vitell's words, "fully present!" Worship, like cooking, requires us to be fully present. It demands our single-hearted attention for it to become the kind of experience that truly provides food for body and soul. In the Lord's kitchen, there are no beeping microwaves, no cardboard disposables, no three minute Ramen Noodle soups, no plastic-wrapped warm ups, no eating while standing over the sink, no quick in and out. In the Lord's kitchen, God seeks a vibrancy of presence, a commitment to the tasks at hand, an exchange of hearts and souls that truly nourishes rather than simply feeds. In the Lord's kitchen, God mixes and mingles, stirs and seasons, sifts and kneads the ingredients of our lives.

The Lord's kitchen is a place in which to draw close, to roll up one's sleeves, to engage all the senses, to fashion and create a meal to be shared by many. When we gather in the sacred space of the Lord's kitchen, we truly are empowered to *Taste and See the Goodness of the Lord!*

# "A FEW, TRIFLING STEPS AHEAD"

*He is not dead, this friend; not dead,*
*Gone some few, trifling steps ahead,*
*And nearer to the end;*
*So that you, too, once past the bend,*
*Shall meet again, as face to face, this friend*
*You fancy dead.*
*(Robert Louis Stevenson)*

In other climes in which I have lived, there was little need for the turn of the calendar page marked "November" in order to know it was here. Bone-chilling winds galloping across the landscape, an occasional flurry or two dropping from the sky, and weighty sweaters and layers of confining clothes all signaled a change—a change that would last, unfortunately, for many months to come. Those early November days, if they could be described in a word, were "raw."

And so are some of the memories conjured by that same flip of the calendar page—memories of my loved ones and friends who have crossed over to a life beyond my own. Even after many, many years, my yearnings for their presence still seem "raw," as though they were as fresh as the coming of this season itself.

At times our losses sneak up on us like a child dressed in a Halloween costume, hoping to make us jump. At times our losses plague us like those surprisingly sleepless nights of tossing and turning when we surely were convinced that we'd drift off the moment our exhausted body hit the mattress. At times our losses stick in our throat so stubbornly that we can hardly swallow what today wants to feed us. At times our losses seem unforgiving and terminal.

The gap, the distance…despite all the remembering and crying and pining we can muster seems so wide, so impenetrable, so unfathomable, that we wonder how we'll ever find our way back to one another.

And all this is happening even as we claim our faith in the Resurrection of Jesus Christ! In our better moments of faith, we claim our losses as heaven's gains, but truth be told, we are jealous that heaven now shares someone we want for ourselves—at least a bit longer than we had him or her.

We long for closeness, some mending of the gap that seems to separate us from our deceased loved ones. The fleeting touches of their presence that occasionally creep into our minds and hearts, sometimes even touching our bodies, seem like "taunts and teases," only stirring up desires for more of them, and with greater frequency.

But it is these very moments of grace, these palpable meetings we have with our beloved dead that remind us that the veil can be thin, and that there are times in the year, ushered in by the very ebb and flow of the seasons of our lives, when the veil of our separation is finer than silk—and we can indeed reach out and touch…and be touched by…our loved ones on the other side of God's Kingdom. In the words of Robert Louis Stevenson, our loved ones are not so discouragingly far beyond, but rather "some few, trifling steps ahead."

Perhaps it is the very "rawness" of this season, which even here in warmer climes, while not scratching at our bodies, still scratches on our souls—that leads us to these "thin places" where heaven and earth are brushing up against each other as gently and softly as a feather upon a baby's cheek.

We, the living, in the "thin places" of this season, are invited to draw close to all the souls who have "gone before us marked with the sign of faith" and to allow the healing power of God to soothe our losses.

Indeed these days may be raw, but therein rests their beauty and power—for it takes a strong, driving, and sometimes relentless force to dismantle the walls of separation we construct in our lives—even those which separate us from the dead.

# A PLACE FOR SPIRITS TO DWELL

*You have died, and your life is hidden with Christ in God. When Christ your life appears, then you too will appear with him in glory (Col. 3:3-4).*

During a summer vacation to a great little hotel only steps away from Tampa Bay, set amongst their lush tropical gardens, I spied a large, carved, temple-like structure sitting atop a thick, wooden mast. The owners of the inn have roots in Thailand, so I suspected it was not only decorative, but perhaps a token reminder of the land they left far behind. Upon closer inspection, I became even more curious as I noted the temple was "populated"! There were tiny figurines, as well as other diminutive objects, occupying the temple precincts. Knowing the owners had no children on property, I quickly dismissed the idea that this was a little girl's elaborate Asian dollhouse.

I now know that this intriguing piece of architecture was in fact a Buddhist "Spirit House." They are as common to the front yards of Thais as windsocks and gazing balls are for Westerners. Made of either wood or stone, with colorful, curving, upward-pointing roof gables and trim, one can find Spirit Houses outside homes and businesses.

And their purpose? The name, "Spirit House," tells the story—they are intended to provide a dwelling place for the "spirits" who live on the land. Like guests who may come to our own homes, Buddhists know some of these spirits to be welcome ones, while others are best kept at a distance—lest they overstay their welcome. So, the Spirit Houses are constructed a "safe" distance from the family home or business in order to preserve the inhabitants from any unwanted visitors or spirits who may choose to overextend their stays!

Buddhists are not the only ones who maintain a connection with spirits—Christians do as well. In fact, the month of November has traditionally been recognized for Catholics as a special time of year, as a special season of remembrance and connection with the saints and souls who have gone before us in faith. While we may not construct Spirit Houses in our front yards or along the walkways of the church, I suspect many of us keep a kind of "Spirit House" in our own hearts and minds where we, like the Buddhists, visit and tend to the spirits of our deceased loved ones.

In the Funeral Liturgy Vigil of the Catholic Church, we invite the bereaved to prayer with these words: ***My sisters***

***and brothers, we believe that all the ties of friendship and affection which knit us as one throughout our lives do not unravel with death.***

Indeed, the prayer we utter gives voice to what we already know, or at least cling to with desperate hope, that with the passage of our loved ones through the doorway of death into new life in Christ, we do not lose them into a dark and unapproachable abyss. We place our faith in a God who would not set us up to forge deep and abiding bonds of love and compassion, only to have them evaporate at the moment of death. Indeed, the prayer we utter gives voice to our sincere hope that our loved ones, the "spirits" who are now released from this life to return home to the Father's many mansions, dwell among us, are approachable in prayer and contemplation, and in many ways, are now bound more closely to us than they were here on earth. While we clearly long to see and touch and experience their presence in the ways we enjoyed before their deaths, we place our confidence in the One whom the Father raised from the dead on Easter morning, and so we hold fast to the belief that the threads of our lives, which become knit together in a beautiful tapestry of loving relationships, are not unraveled and discarded by the hand of death.

We may not build "Spirit Houses" of wood and stone for all to see, but I surely know that I have constructed many in the depth of my own heart—and therein, I make a place and often invite the spirits of grandparents and colleagues, friends and neighbors, mentors and guides to stop on occasion. In the quiet of this sacred dwelling space, I welcome the spirits of Emma and Diane, Dru and Freddy, Sal and Fran, Larry and Bill to reminisce, to encourage, to reinvigorate, and to embrace—perhaps not as I would fully desire to see and know them again—but as palpable and true as I will ever know on this side of eternity.

May each of us spend this month of November building up our own little "Spirit Houses" so that all the faithful departed, whose loss we continue to mourn, and whom we deeply desire to see and cherish again, may dwell among us a welcome visitors.

# THE POTTER'S FIELD:
## *"NO KNOWN FAMILY"*

As I approached the man in the tailored suit, idly chatting away with another fellow already sweaty and dirty from the day's work, the name "Joe" stitched to his well-worn, drab uniform shirt, I introduced myself, and was handed a crumbled piece of blue scrap paper. It simply read: "Kenneth Brown, age 38 of Orlando, died on June 30, 2001. Born on Oct 13, 1962 in Deleware (sic). No known family."

This was my introduction to Ken Brown, the man for whom I was about to offer funeral prayers, as his stark, modest casket and vault were about to be lowered into the Orange County Cemetery, a little plot of land tucked at the back end of a sprawling, well-manicured, and marble monument-filled corporate cemetery, where the County's indigents are buried.

I had never been called out to a service in this place, so I carefully followed the directions I was given. I mistakenly drove into the larger cemetery, and after winding my way amongst the grave markers and monuments, I realized that I was no closer to my destination. After stopping at the office, and receiving what turned out to be inaccurate directions, I was able to spy a backhoe and casket perched in the middle of a green field just beyond the fence where I parked the car. Now it was a simple case of "I know where I need to go; but how do I get from here to there?!" Knocking on the door of a dilapidated trailer, a kind lady was able to give much better directions than my previous contact, and I proceeded out of the cemetery and onto the dirt road that would lead me to Kenneth Brown.

The heavily pot-holed dirt road, its craters filled with standing water and muck, would have been better navigated by a Quad or Humvee rather than my Honda Accord. As I slowly made my way, driving past a couple of beautiful horses standing in their owner's front yard, I had the overwhelming feeling that I was entering into the middle of a deeply held, closely guarded secret. Everything from the easily missed entrance, to this swatch of dirt, to the precarious obstacle course drive along its path, seemed to smack of "Stay Out!" "Enter At You Own Risk!" (In fact, I had heard, previous to the day of the service, that indeed no one was permitted to visit this cemetery lot for the poor, and that it was highly unusual for clergy to come to the graveside).

Passing through the open gate, I spied the funeral director and the grave digger, and parked my car, fearful that any further driving onto the field might find my car hermetically sealed in mud. Fortunately, our methodical afternoon summer rains had decided to allow me the grace to complete my task before letting loose another day's welcome soaking.

As I slowly made my first trip across what is known, in common parlance, as a "Potter's Field," I wondered how may lonely and forgotten souls, infants and elderly, and all those in between, were buried beneath my feet. In the "Potter's Field," there are no grave markers (that is, until recently), not even the simple recognition of the name the person bore in this life—no identity, no distinction, no dignity.

I had never met Kenneth Brown. My presence on this day was simply a response to a plea from a local nursing home chaplain. In the final days of his earthly life, Ken Brown uttered his dying wish—that a Catholic priest would be at his side to offer burial prayers. Thc apostle Paul's words became vivid, as recounted in the *General Introduction to the Christian Order of Funerals:*

*If one member suffers in the body of Christ which is the Church, all the members suffer with that member (1 Cor. 12:26). For this reason, those who are baptized into Christ and nourished at the same table of the Lord are responsible for one another.*

Obviously not easily mistaken for an unauthorized intruder (my clerical collar giving me away on first glance), the funeral director greeted me, and pressed the crumpled piece of paper, torn from an unused "Memorial Card," into my hand, as though he were passing a secret code message. He asked if I would like to "see" Mr. Brown, and I responded with a gentle, "Please, if it's not too difficult to open the casket." Over the years of my ministry, I have discovered both the need and desire to "see" the people over whom I offer the Church's funeral rites. When I am unable to do so, for a variety of practical reasons, I feel as though I have not been able to make a connection with them, to somehow touch the "beloved of God" who now is returned home to our Creator.

In the moment or two that I gazed at Ken Brown's face, the stark reality of his death overwhelmed me, and I wondered not so much about his death, but rather about his life—who he had been, what twists and turns his life had taken, what illnesses ravaged him, and most especially, how he had come to be a person "with no known family."

Ken Brown was the second man I have looked upon in death in recent months who looked more like 58 rather than 38. (The first man being "Troy," a local transient, whom I witnessed being killed by a hit-and-run driver on Colonial Drive one night on my way home from locking the church). Without the benefit of his life story, I still surmised that Ken's days were replete with struggle. His weathered face and sunken eyes unabashedly spoke out like pages of a tragic novel, heavily creased with sorrow and pain. While his face did bear small signs of scratches and scrapes, somehow, deep down, beyond the physical evidence, I know him to be a man whom life had beaten and tossed to the side of any number of paths, not unlike the "road going down from Jerusalem to Jericho," where so many of God's beloved creations lay bleeding and wounded, desperately clinging to the hope that a Samaritan, rather than a priest or Levite might pass their way.

While awaiting the arrival of the Orange County official responsible for making sure everything was legitimate, the three of us engaged in the usual banter that people make while standing around a coffin—the weather, the history of the cemetery, plans for the weekend, the dropping price of gas. I tried not to appear aloof from the conversation, but my mind and heart were little concerned with visions of weekend revelry and gas prices. I wanted Ken to have some token of dignity, some modicum of the grace and compassion that most people and their families are offered on the day of their burial. As the *Order of Christian Funerals* reminds us:

*At the death of a Christian, whose life of faith was begun in the waters of baptism and strengthened at the Eucharistic table, the Church intercedes on behalf of the deceased....*

And above all, I couldn't help but think, why? Why this? Why this way? And the words from the paper, misspelling and all, kept echoing in my ears like a plaintive, sorrowful dirge: *"No known family!" "No known family!" "No known family!"*

This, to me, is the greatest tragedy of Ken Brown's life and death. At a mere 38 years old, how does one have "no known family," or for that matter apparently, "no known friends"?

After completing the ritual prayers of our faith, I stayed long enough to see Ken Brown's casket and vault lowered into the ground. While we often refer to one's grave site as his or her "final resting place," I know better. While we honor our earthly dwelling with Christian burial, our true "final resting place" is not some hole in the ground, but rather a heavenly banquet table, around which are gathered all of God's loved ones; and those with seats near the head of the table are the lost and forsaken of this world, those for whom God reserves a special comfort and peace, because "God hears the cry of the poor!"

As I made my way back to the car, a sprinkle or two now descending from the previously cooperative sky, I began to think of all the people in my acquaintance, all those whom I have met, and continue to meet even now in my ministry, who daily make choices to cut themselves off from family. I will never know what happened in Kenneth Brown's life to lead him to a death- walk unaccompanied by family and friends. Perhaps he made those same choices I see and hear people making now. Perhaps he uttered one too many times the same refrain I hear from others: "No one understands me; I'd be better off without them!" "All my family has ever done is get in the way of my happiness, my success, my dreams, my hopes—I'd be better off without them!" "My family has brought me nothing but misery and aggravation; I hate them! I'll be glad when they leave me alone!" "No one has ever done anything for me—I've had to earn everything myself; I might as well keep to myself!" And on and on....

Perhaps Kenneth Brown, or perhaps the people who knew him, who once were family and friends, had come to the end of their ropes, could no longer keep the bonds of family and friendship intact—and either cut one another loose, or were too exhausted to tie them together again.

Whatever the case, I can't help but continue to see in my mind's eye, even as I write these words, the utter aloneness and pain, the wounds and brokenness etched upon the stone-cold face of a man who died and was buried without the comfort and companionship of family and friends.

From the perspective of our faith tradition, in reality, Kenneth Brown, age 38 of Orlando, born in Delaware in 1962, does have family—the family of God, the family of the Church. *"If one member suffers in the body of Christ which is the Church, all the members suffer with that member."* This is the gift of baptism! My presence on the day of his burial was testimony and witness to this reality. Yet, the family he needed, the family he deserved as a human being, the family we all need, had faded from his life, and left him to die alone.

*"The Church through its funeral rites commends the dead to God's merciful love and pleads for the forgiveness of their sins"*

*(Order of Christian Funerals)*. On that lonely, muddy field, shielded from our view and blotted from anyone's memories, I trusted in God's mercy and pleaded for the forgiveness of Kenneth Brown's sins...of my sins...of our sins—all the sins that lead us to abandon one another.

Perhaps, as our feet carry us further today along our own life's pilgrimage, we might offer a prayer for Kenneth Brown...and we might reconsider our own family bonds—those for which we are deeply grateful, as well as those for which we are in need of healing and reconciliation. It is surely a tragedy that anyone should live and die alone; it is a far greater tragedy when we choose to make that a possibility.

*May his soul and all the souls of the faithful departed, through the mercy of God, rest in peace! Amen!*

# A FINAL WORD ON WORDS
# "BE CAREFUL WHAT YOU SAY!"

My reading of their essays aroused a classic, but friendly argument that I always had each semester with several of my college students. No matter what the subject or assigned topic happened to be, the problem reared its head any time pen was put to paper (or better to say, any time finger was put to keyboard).

The arguments went something like this. I would read the essay; comment upon my inability to understand what they were trying to say; make a suggestion or two about another way of expressing themselves; and sometimes question if they truly understood what they were discussing. In return, after reviewing their "bloody" essay (yes, I used a cold-hearted RED pen for commentary) and sharing with me their pain and disappointment over their assigned grade, they would inevitably say: "But that's not what I *meant* to say; I really wanted to say this…." To which I would respond: "Well, I'm happy that was your *intention*—problem is, that's not what you actually did write!"

Seems we all struggle with a clear way to articulate what we mean. Whether writing an essay, sending someone a card or note, sitting down over a mocha latte and sharing our joys or sorrows, having a heart-to-heart with a child over his or her recent disobedience, or giving expression to our deepest longings to God—we don't always seem to be able to express what we truly mean, what we truly want to say. Often, like my former students, there's a robust gap between what we "mean to say" and how it actually comes out!

Words have a life of their own once they leave our lips or flow onto paper. We need to be careful with them—both how we deliver them and how we receive them.

I have attempted, with great care, to use words in these *Firestarters* in a way that respects the people and experiences I share with you. I may not have always communicated what I truly wanted to say, but the fact is, now I *have* said it, written it, and it is with a gracious and understanding heart I invite you to receive it.

From the moment that God first "spoke" and creation was underway, words have been sacred—despite our continuing corruption of their beauty. May the words within these pages, and those yet to come in future *Firestarters,* ignite a fire for the Sacred who dwells above, behind, beneath, beside and within all that is seen and unseen—all that is spoken and unspoken.

LaVergne, TN USA
09 March 2011
219183LV00001B/1/P

9 781432 769444